DATA LAKE

ARCHITECTURE

Designing the Data Lake
and
Avoiding the Garbage
Dump

first edition

Bill Inmon

Published by:

2 Lindsley Road
Basking Ridge, NJ 07920 USA

https://www.TechnicsPub.com

Cover design by John Fiorentino
Edited by R A Peters

Copyright © 2016 by Bill Inmon

ISBN, print ed.	9781634621175
ISBN, Kindle ed.	9781634621182
ISBN, ePub ed.	9781634621199
ISBN, PDF ed.	9781634621205

First Printing 2016

Library of Congress Control Number: 2016935768

To Dr. Sylvia Sydow,
you mean the world to me

Contents at a Glance

Table of Contents

Introduction

We invest millions of dollars and years of time to build it wrong, but can't we spare a dime or a minute to build it right?

Nowadays corporations are madly building data lakes, a by-product of the Big Data mania. Then one day they wake up and find that they can't get anything meaningful out of their data lake. Or at least it takes a monumental effort to get the smallest amount of useful information out of their data lake.

They spend huge amounts of money and many man years of effort and build something that is a white elephant.

One day the corporation wakes up to the fact that they have built a "one way" data lake. Data goes into the data lake but nothing ever comes out. When this happens, the data lake is no more useful than a garbage dump.

This book is dedicated to corporations that want to build data lakes so that they *can* get useful information out of their data lakes. There is business value in the data lake, but only if you build it properly. If you are going to build a data lake you may as well build it so that it becomes an important corporate asset, not a liability.

The book examines why corporations have such a hard time getting anything useful out of their data lakes. There are several answers to this important question. One reason is that data is just packed into the data lake in an indiscriminant fashion. Another answer is that data is not integrated. A third reason is that data is stored in a textual manner and you can't easily do analysis on text.

This book suggests that a high level of organization of data in the data lake is needed and that integration and "conditioning" of the integrated data is needed in order to make the data a foundation for analytical processing. The data lake can be turned into a positive asset for the corporation, but only if there is care and forethought in the shaping of the data lake.

The data lake needs to be divided into several sections, called data ponds. There is the:

- Raw data pond
- Analog data pond
- Application data pond
- Textual data pond
- Archival data pond.

After the data ponds are created, the ponds require conditioning in order to make the data accessible and useful. For example, the analog data pond needs to have data reduction and data compression applied to it. The application data pond needs to have classical ETL integration applied to it. The textual data pond needs to have textual disambiguation applied to the text so that the text can be reduced to a uniform database structure and so that the context of the text can be identified.

Once the data ponds have had conditioning algorithms applied to their data, the data ponds then serve as a basis for analytical processing. Once the data in the data lake has been divided into ponds and the ponds have their data conditioned, then the ponds serve as an asset for the corporation, not a liability. In addition the data in the ponds is moved to the archival data pond when the useful life of the data in the data pond is over.

This book is for managers, students, system developers, architects, programmers, and end users. This book is designed to be a guideline to the organization that wishes to build data lakes that are an asset, not a liability.

Chapter 1
Data Lakes

First came the punch card. Then magnetic tapes. Then disk storage and database management systems, followed by fourth generation languages (4GLs), "metadata" and floppy disks and mobile computing. Advances coming faster than we could memorize their new names. Soon personal computers and spreadsheets became as ubiquitous as suits and ties. And that was just the beginning.

In a rapid few decades, the corporation went from no automation to hyper automation. Throughout this progression one of the limiting factors was storage. Storage was always either too expensive or too limited in its capacity to hold large volumes of data. The bottleneck of storage limits had a profound effect on the types of systems that could be built and hampered the performance of systems that were built.

ENTER BIG DATA

Then one day Big Data changed the world. Big Data technology was best typified by the Hadoop Distributed File System (HDFS). This open-source software framework was designed from the ground up to store and process massive datasets distributed among many different computer clusters. With Big Data, storage is effectively unlimited in terms of cost and technical constraints. Most importantly, with Big Data whole new worlds of processing and opportunity opened up.

In short order, Big Data redefined our very conception of data. The sheer volume of data that could be stored and analyzed with Big Data systems revolutionized not just the industry, but the world. Megabytes, gigabytes, terabytes... the old data measures were thrown out the window in this new world where storage volume was effectively unlimited. Fig 1.1 depicts the advent of Big Data.

Big Data

Fig 1.1 Creating unlimited opportunities by leveraging Big Data

ENTER THE DATA LAKE

As Big Data blossomed, organizations began to store the endless stream of data being collected in structures called "data lakes."

While collecting the data was a piece of cake, plucking something useful from this sea of knowledge was the real challenge. Some organizations turned to data scientists to make sense out of their data lakes. Despite the costs sunk into research, Big Data was just as brand new and unexplored for the scientists as the organizations. Analytic breakthroughs were rare, expensive to produce and fraught with false positives and other errors. Fig 1.2 shows that Big Data leads to massive data lakes to sift through.

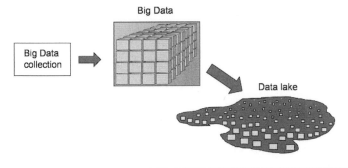

Fig 1.2 Placing Big Data in the data lake

Fig 1.3 shows the frustration by the business community that grew as the volume, and therefore value, of data in the data lake continued to grow, while they could do little of value with their treasure.

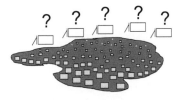

Fig 1.3 Waking up and finding that we can't find anything in the data lake

"ONE WAY" DATA LAKE

There were many reasons for business users to be frustrated with the information pooling in their data lakes. The core issue was that the larger the information lake grew, the more difficult analyzing the data became. A data lake of any significant size was often dubbed a "one way lake," since data is eternally pouring in, but data and/or any analysis is never taken out, or even accessed once the data is placed inside the data lake. Fig 1.4 depicts the "one way" data lake.

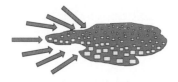

Fig 1.4 Entering data into the "one way" data lake, but nothing comes out

It was an expensive and frustrating Catch-22. The larger and more potentially insightful a data lake grew, the more useless it became to the organization. If no one is using data in the data lake, then the lake serves no purpose to the organization. Yet the organization was paying a lot of money on storage and the specialized staff to extract useful information out of the data lake.

The question then arose – why is the data lake one way and what can be done about it? There is great potential in Big Data and data lakes, but no one seems to be getting their money's worth out of their investment. There are many reasons why the data lake turns into a "one way" data lake. But those issues trace their roots to how data was placed into the data lake in the first place: the intent was never to organize the data for future usage. Instead the data lake became a place just to "dump" data. So much effort was spent on gathering data from every possible source that few engineers or companies gave much thought to organizing the data for future usage. Fig 1.5 shows that with the "one way" data lake, the lake becomes little more than a large garbage dump for data.

Fig 1.5 Turning the data lake into a garbage dump

Does the data lake have to become a garbage dump? Isn't there something that can be done in order to make the data lake a productive and useful place? Were the promises of Big Data just a bunch of hype by the vendor? Indeed, the data lake has the potential to become a quite useful foundation for analytical processing. However, as long as people simply dump data into the data lake with little or no thought to the future usage of the data, then the data lake is destined to remain a garbage dump.

What are some of the issues with the data lake when data is merely dumped inside? Let's unpack the core problems one by one.

One issue is that useful data becomes hidden from the analyst because it is buried behind mountains of other information that are not relevant. There is nothing very remarkable about much of the data that is useful to companies. And given the sheer volume of data found in the data lake, the blandness of useful data makes it that much more difficult to find. Put another way, useful data just doesn't stand out in the mountains of data that accumulate in the data lake.

A second and related issue is that the metadata describing the data points in the data lake are not captured or stored in an accessible location. Only the raw data is stored in the data lake. This makes analysis of data a really dicey issue because the analyst never knows the meaning or source of the data that has found its way into the data lake. In order to perform useful analysis, the organization needs accurate and readily accessible metadata that puts the data found in the data lake in context.

A third shortcoming of the one-way data lake is that data relationships are lost (or are never even recognized). The pool is so large that important data relationships are not carried forward into the data lake. It's considered too cumbersome to carry data relationships into the data lake.

And this list is just the beginning of the shortcomings of data in a "one way" data lake. In fact, there are many more technical obstacles in the way of effectively utilizing a data lake. Fig 1.6 shows some of the limitations of data in the data lake.

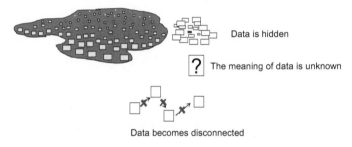

Data is hidden

The meaning of data is unknown

Data becomes disconnected

Fig 1.6 Traditionally analyzing data in the data lake becomes impossible

IN SUMMARY

Because the information inside the data lake is not designed for future access and analysis, the organization soon discovers the data lake will not support their business, no matter how large it is.

Organizations have long known that in order to support the business, data must be organized in a rational, easy to use, and easy to understand manner. Due to data being dumped into the lake with no thought for future usage, the data lake is consequently not useful to the business.

When the data lake is transformed into a "one way" data lake, the only benefit to the business of the data lake is as a cheap facility for the storage of useless data. The data lake as a cheap form of storage hardly justifies the expense and investment organizations have made.

So let's take a look at solutions for this quandary.

Chapter 2
Transforming the Data Lake

The data lake has great potential. The data lake can be used to conduct analytical processing that has never before been done. From governments to small businesses, the data lake can be used to identify, analyze and even predict important patterns which heretofore have gone unnoticed.

What needs to be done to turn the data lake into an information gold mine? What exactly does the organization need to think about as it creates its data lake? What are the things that can be done to data that will prepare for future usage and analysis?

With care and planning, the data lake can be turned into an information gold mine. What are the ingredients that are needed to turn the data lake into a bottomless well of actionable insights? There are four basic ingredients that are needed: metadata, integration mapping, context, and metaprocess.

METADATA

Metadata is the description of the data in the data lake itself (as opposed to the raw data). Metadata is the basic structural information that every collection of data has associated with it. For example, if tracking visits, clicks and engagement to a website, metadata would include the IP address/geographic location of the visiting computer.

Typical forms of metadata include descriptions of the record, the attributes, the keys, the indexes and the relationships among the different attributes of data. There are however many additional forms of metadata.

Metadata is used by the analyst to decipher the raw data found in the data lake. Or in other words, metadata is the basic roadmap of the data that resides in the data lake.

When only raw data is stored in the data lake, the analyst that needs to use that data is crippled. Imagine trying to search Wikipedia if none of the articles had titles. Raw data by itself just isn't very useful. Now when raw data is properly tagged with metadata and stored in the data lake together, you now have an incredibly useful service.

INTEGRATION MAPPING

The integration map describes how data from one application relates to data from another application and how that data can be meaningfully combined. As important as metadata is, it is not the only basic infrastructure ingredient needed in the data lake. Consider that most of the data lake's input is generated by an application, in one form or the other. What happens when you put data from different applications in the data lake? You create unintegrated "silos" of data in the data lake.

Each application, usually written in a different coding language, sends its input to a separate silo, which cannot communicate or "talk to" the other silos. While the information is all stored in the same data lake, each silo is unable to integrate its data with the others, even if properly tagged with metadata.

In order to make sense of the data in the data lake, it is necessary to create an "integration map." The integration map is a detailed specification that shows how the lake's data can be integrated. The integration map is the best method to overcome the isolation of data in the silos.

Fig 2.1 shows that when unintegrated application data is placed in the data lake, silos of data are created. These silos make the reading and interpretation of data a very difficult thing to do.

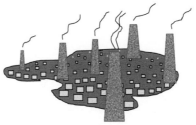

Fig 2.1 Creating silos leads to unintegrated data, hindering communication

CONTEXT

Another complicating factor in the data lake is textual data that has been placed there without context of the text being identified. Suppose the text "court" appears. Does court refer to a tennis court? To a legal proceeding? To the activities of a young man as he tries to lure a young lady as his mate? Does court refer to the people surrounding royalty? When you look at the word "court" by itself, it might mean any of these things or more.

Text without context is meaningless data. In fact, in some cases it is dangerous to store text without an understanding of its context. If you are going to put text in the data lake, then you must also insert context as well, or at least a way to find that context. Fig 2.2 shows that context for text is an essential ingredient for data found in the data lake.

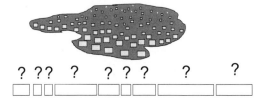

Fig 2.2 Lacking context of textual data

METAPROCESS

Metaprocess information is information about how the data was processed or how the information in the data lake will be processed. When was the data generated? Where was the data generated? How much data was generated? Who generated the data? How was the data selected to be placed in the data lake? Once inside the data lake, was the data further processed? All of these forms of metaprocessing are useful to the analyst as they go about extracting and analyzing the lake's data.

The most important point is that these features need to be included at the outset. Usually, after the raw data has been loaded into the data lake, it is too late to go back and include these essential ingredients.

However, once the ingredients have been added, the data lake is a potential information gold mine. Fig 2.3 depicts the broad strokes required to turn the data lake into a powerful and useful corporate resource.

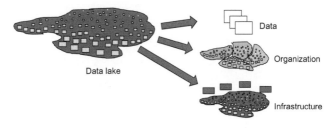

Figure 2.3 Going from a garbage dump to an information gold mine

Another important effect of turning the data lake into a useful corporate resource is that an entirely different and expanded community of users can make use of the tool.

Consider the transformation of a data lake into a useful corporate resource. Fig 2.4 shows the data lake in an untransformed state and the data lake in a transformed state.

Fig 2.4 Going from an untransformed state into a transformed state

DATA SCIENTIST

When the data lake is in its raw state only a handful of specialists can make sense of the data in the data lake. Typically these people are called data scientists. Data scientists are:

- Hard to find

- Expensive to hire
- Hard to get their time when they are hired.

There is nothing wrong with data scientists as a group of people. But the difficulty in even finding them, the cost of hiring them, and the difficulty in getting their time even when they are found and hired is legendary. No matter how well organized, when the data lake can be operated only by a few people whose cost is high and time is precious, the data lake just has limited corporate value.

GENERAL USABILITY

Now consider what happens when the data lake is fully integrated and the data is transformed into a state of general usability.

Fig 2.5 shows the difference between a data lake that is accessible only to a few data scientists and one after transformation that's accessible to a large population of business users.

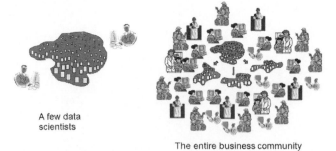

A few data
scientists

The entire business community

Fig 2.5 Transforming data increases user accessibility

After transformation, the data lake is useful to accountants, managers, systems analysts, the end user, the finance team, sales staff, marketing and so forth. By integrating and conditioning the data, the audience served by the data lake expands greatly. And in doing so, the lake's value to the corporation expands greatly.

IN SUMMARY

The data lake has great potential. But when people merely dump data inside with no thought as to how the data will be used, there is the very real danger that the data lake will turn into a garbage dump. With four basic ingredients, the data lake can be turned into an information gold mine:

- **Metadata**. Metadata is used by the analyst to decipher the raw data found in the data lake. Metadata is the basic roadmap of data that resides in the data lake.

- **Integration mapping**. The integration map is a detailed specification that shows how the data in the data lake can be integrated. The integration map shows how the isolation of data in the silos can be overcome.

- **Context**. If you are going to put text in the data lake, then you must also insert context as well, or at least a way to find that context.

- **Metaprocess**. Metaprocess tags are information about the processing of data in the data lake.

Chapter 3
Inside the Data Lake

In order to better understand how the data lake can be prepared for future access and analysis, it is necessary to take a look at what lies inside the data lake.

While it is true that *any* kind of data can be found inside the data lake, it is nevertheless possible to categorize the data into three categories:

- Analog data
- Application data
- Textual data.

Fig 3.1 shows that most data inside the data lake fits into one of three categories.

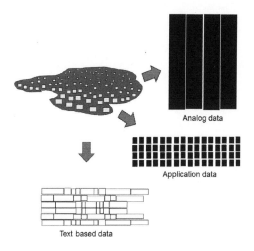

Analog data

Application data

Text based data

Fig 3.1 Categorizing data lake data into three types

ANALOG DATA

The first type of data found in the data lake is analog data. Analog data is typically generated by a machine or some other automated device, even if not connected to the internet. These measuring tools include diagnostic programs logging performance on everything from nuclear reactors to the CPU usage of your mobile phone.

In general, analog data is very voluminous and very repetitive. Most analog data consists of a long list of numbers that have been generated. Most records created by an analog device are measurements and most of the time those measurements only vary slightly from all other measurements. Typically, these small outliers are of the most interest.

Analog data usually are a simple measurement of some physical value (heat, weight, chemical composition, size, etc.). When a measurement seems out of line, it is an indication to look elsewhere for the cause of the measurement. For example, the odd measurement may have been caused by the fact that a machine has lost its calibration. Or a part needs an adjustment, and so forth. The analog data is merely a signal to the analyst to look elsewhere as to the cause of the variation in measurement.

Which is why the metaprocess information associated with analog data is often times more important than the analog data itself. Metaprocess details typically include such information as time of measurement, location of measurement, speed of measurement, and so forth.

Typically, analog information is triggered by or associated with some trigger, such as a manufacturing event. A part is created. A shipment has been sent. A box has been moved. These are all common events causing the creation of an analog record. The analog measurement is almost always made mechanically, without any user input or extra processing. Fig 3.2 shows an event triggering the creation of an analog measurement.

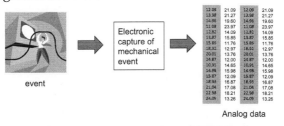

Fig 3.2 Triggering analog measurements through events

The data points accompanying the raw data captured in the analog measurement process is called "metaprocess" data. While there are different kinds of metaprocess models suited to different objectives, this raw output is the most relevant to data lakes. The metaprocess information provides a different perspective of the analog data than just looking at the raw data itself. Fig 3.3 depicts some typical metaprocess details.

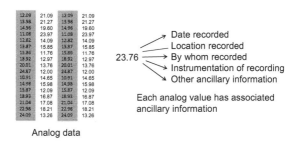

Fig 3.3 Providing a different perspective of the analog data than just looking at the raw data itself

Often times the analog measurements are stored in log tapes or journal tapes. A log tape is a sequential measurement of one or more variables detected during the event(s) that creates an analog measurement. A log tape is very detailed. Numbers are generated in very small intervals.

The format of the log tape is typically complex. Often times system utilities are used to read and interpret the log tape because of their complexity. In most cases, the log tape captures *all* the events that occur, not just the events that are of interest or events that are an exception. As a consequence, it's normal for a log tape to contain much extraneous information. Fig 3.4 shows the analog data found on a normal log tape.

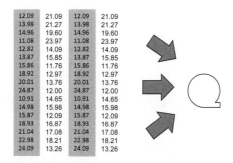

Fig 3.4 Storing analog data in log tapes or journals

APPLICATION DATA

The second general category of data found in data lakes is application data. Application data is generated by the execution of an application or transaction, and sent to the data lake. As important as transaction data is, it is not the only kind of data found in the application component of the data lake.

Typical types of application data found in the data lake include sales data, payment data, banking checking data, manufacturing process control data, shipment data, contract completion data, inventory management data, billing data, bill payment data, and so forth. When any business relevant event occurs, the event is measured by an application and the data is created.

The physical manifestation of application data in the data lake can take many forms. However, the most typical form is recording activity in an application. The records may or may not have been shaped by a database management system (DBMS) application. It is typical of the application records to have a common and repeating uniform structure. Fig 3.5 shows that structure.

Fig 3.5 Repeating the same structure

The common, uniform structure of the application data is usually in the form of a record, which is more than an analog data point. The record may have attributes. One or more of those attributes may be designated as a key. One or more of the attributes can have an independent index. Fig 3.6 shows the key and record structure that is typical of application data in the data lake.

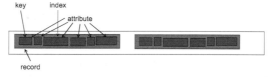

Fig 3.6 Typical key and record structure in the data lake

It is noteworthy that the structure of application data may or may not be rigorously tied to the DBMS that the data once was housed in.

TEXTUAL DATA

The third general type of data found in the data lake is textual data. The textual data is usually associated with an application. However, the textual data takes a very different form than application data. Whereas application data is shaped into uniform records, data found in a textual format is decidedly not shaped into any uniform form.

Textual data is called "unstructured data" because the text can take any form. For example, when a person is speaking, they can say anything in any fashion that they like. Usually the sounds make sense, but many variables can strip away the structure. They could speak in riddles and parables. They might use a different language. Their speech may contain slang, vulgarities, be in a formal style or might even be an inside joke. Naturally, such text is extremely content dependent and not easily searched or processed by automated means.

Typical text found in corporations include call center conversations, corporate contracts, email, insurance claims, sales pitches, court orders, jokes, tweets, invitations and so forth. There is no limit as to what kind of text and how much text can be stored in a data lake. However, in order for text to be used analytically it must be transformed. As long as text is in its original form, only the most superficial analysis can be done against the text. In order for text to be subjected to useful analytical processing, unstructured text must pass through a process known as textual disambiguation.

Note that analog data and application data rarely have to pass through a similar process. Because of the uniformity with which analog data and application data are captured, those kinds of data points are expected to be analyzed by a computer. But if there is to be exhaustive analysis of text, it must be passed from its unstructured form of data through textual disambiguation at which point it passes into a state and form that can be analyzed by the computer.

There are two principal activities that are accomplished by textual disambiguation:

- Text goes from an unstructured state to a structured uniform state that can be analyzed by the computer, and
- Text has context recognized and associated with the text itself.

While these are the two primary functions of textual disambiguation, there are other useful functions accomplished by textual disambiguation. The most complex of these disambiguation activities is the identification of the context of text and the association of text with that context, as seen in Fig 3.7.

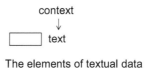

The elements of textual data

Fig 3.7 Identifying the context of text

ANOTHER PERSPECTIVE

The three major categories of data found in the data lake then are analog data, application data and textual data. But there is another important classification of data in the data lake between repetitive and non-repetitive data. In general, analog and application data are repetitive, whereas textual data is non repetitive. Fig 3.8 shows data in the data lake divided into classifications of repetitive data and non-repetitive data.

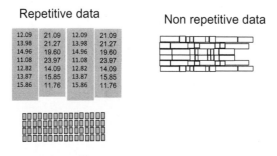

Fig 3.8 Repetitive data is data where the same unit of data occurs over and over. Non-repetitive data is data where the same unit of data does not occur repeatedly, if at all.

While this might seem minor at first glance, there is great significance to the division of data into these two classifications.

In later chapters, we will explore the differences between repetitive and non-repetitive data in terms of business value and the significance of this division. Generally, there is great business value in non-repetitive data while significantly less business value is found in repetitive data. Because of the stark difference in business value, they form what is called the "great divide" between the two types of data, as seen in Fig 3.9.

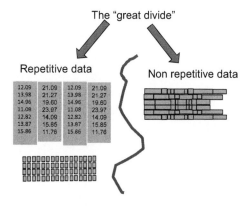

Fig 3.9 The "great divide" between repetitive and non-repetitive data

IN SUMMARY

There are many ways of organizing a data lake. One of those ways is to categorize data into one of three categories:

- Analog data
- Application data
- Textual data.

Another important method of categorizing data is into repetitive and non-repetitive data. The difference between repetitive data and non-repetitive data forms what is termed the "great divide."

Chapter 4
Data Ponds

In order to organize the different types of data into a structure that can be analyzed, it is necessary to create a high-level structure of data within the data lake. As data enters the lake it first enters the raw data pond. The purpose of the raw data pond is to serve as a holding cell. There is little or no analysis or other organized activity of the data while in the raw data pond.

Once it is time for analysis, the information in the raw data pond is sent to one of three different ponds based on the kind of data entailed. For example, analog, application and textual data all require a unique data pond.

While it is important to separate the three types of data, once inside the pond considerable processing takes place. It's noteworthy that very different kinds of data processing or conditioning of the data occur inside the data pond. After the conditioning in finished, the data in the pond is fit for analysis.

After the data has outlived its useful life in the data pond, it's moved from the analog, application, or textual pond into an archival data pond. This high-level flow of data from the raw data pond through the analog pond, the application pond, or the textual pond is seen in Fig 4.1.

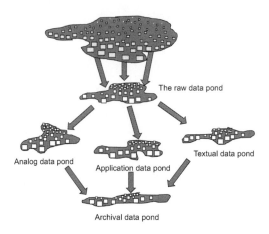

The raw data pond

Analog data pond

Application data pond

Textual data pond

Archival data pond

Fig 4.1 Understanding the data lifecycle across the different types of ponds

CONDITIONING DATA

As data enters the various source ponds, the raw data goes through a conditioning process to prepare the data for analytical processing. Stated differently, if raw data does not go through the conditioning process, it has a hard time supporting the business analysis, which in turn creates business value. This is because the information is not in a format which is easy, or sometimes even possible, to study. It is absolutely mandatory that raw data be conditioned if it is to be fit for supporting analytical processing.

But conditioning for each type of pond is *very* different.

RAW DATA POND

The genesis of data is the raw data pond. The raw data pond is what many organizations initially call the data lake. Too often, they'll simply throw data into the lake and then wonder why they can't do any meaningful analytic processing against the data. In fairness, analytical processing *can* be done against raw data in the data lake. It just requires a data scientist to do the analysis. But much more lucid and efficient data analysis can be done against data after it has been conditioned. Almost as important, once the data has been conditioned, it can then be analyzed by the ordinary business user.

An interesting architectural question is: once raw data flows from the raw data pond into the data pond, should the raw data remain in the raw data pond? The answer is no. Once raw data passes from the raw data pond to the analog data pond, the application data pond, or the textual data pond, it is best to remove the source data from the raw data pond. The raw data has already served its purpose and it would be extremely rare for analytical processing to ever be performed in the raw data pond. The raw data pond then becomes a "holding cell" for a jumble of data, as seen in Fig 4.2.

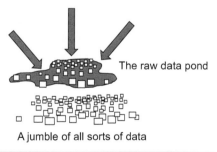

The raw data pond

A jumble of all sorts of data

Fig 4.2 Becoming a "holding cell" for a jumble of data

The data in the raw data pond should be passed to the supporting data ponds as quickly as possible. One useful measure of quality for the raw data pond is how small it is and how quickly data passes out of the pond.

ANALOG DATA POND

The analog data pond is a place where, naturally enough, analog data is stored. The conditioning process for analog data primarily consists of data reduction – of reducing the volume of data in the analog pond to a workable, manageable, meaningful volume of data and restructuring the data in the pond.

APPLICATION DATA POND

The application data pond is populated with information that comes from executing one or more applications. This application data is probably the "cleanest" in the data lake because it has been generated by an application. All the data in the application pond is uniformly structured and contains values that are relevant to the execution of some business activity. But the data in the application pond is notoriously unintegrated. If, by some chance, all the information in this pond comes from a single application, the data in this pond may actually be integrated. However, for large corporations (and it is mostly large corporations who have data lakes) there is a good chance that data in this pond comes from different applications. It's this multi-application origin of data that gives the analyst a hard time.

TEXTUAL DATA POND

The textual data pond is where unstructured textual data is placed. Text here can come from anywhere. Text in this pond is notoriously difficult to analyze in a profound fashion. Text can have a superficial analysis done with no transformation, but in order to do a deep analysis of the data it is necessary to disambiguate the text.

The disambiguation of text has two important effects:

- Text is restructured into a uniform, database format, and
- Text has context identified and attached to the text itself.

DATA PASSING DIRECTLY INTO THE DATA PONDS

It is worthy of note that data does not have to pass through the raw data pond, although it almost always does. If the developer is sophisticated, it is possible to send the data directly into the analog, application or the textual pond of data. However most data passes through the raw data pond simply because that is the way most organizations did it in the beginning. Fig 4.3 shows that raw data can pass directly into the analog, application or textual data pond.

Analog data pond

Application data pond

Textual data pond

Fig 4.3 Sending raw data into the different data ponds

In the final stages of the life cycle of data, data passes from the analog, application or textual data pond into the archival pond.

ARCHIVAL DATA POND

Fig 4.4 shows the passage of data from the various data ponds into the archival data pond.

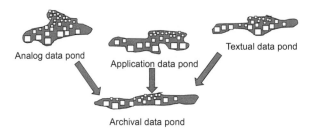

Analog data pond

Application data pond

Textual data pond

Archival data pond

Fig 4.4 Storing data in the archival data pond in optional

The purpose of the archival data pond is to hold data that is not actively needed for analysis but might be needed at some future point in time for analysis.

IN SUMMARY

The data lake that can support analytical processing is divided into several data ponds:

- The raw data pond is the place where data first enters the data lake. The raw data pond serves as a holding cell for data.
- The analog data pond is the place where analog data is channeled.
- The application data pond is the place where application data is channeled.
- The textual data pond is the place where textual data is gathered.

Upon entering the different data ponds, raw data passes through a conditioning process. Finally, when data has reached the end of its useful life, data passes into an archival data pond.

Chapter 5
Generic Structure of the Data Pond

Each of the data ponds (other than the raw data pond) has some common components:

- **Pond descriptor.** The pond descriptor contains a description of the external contents and manifestation of the pond, and where the data in the pond originated from.
- **Pond target.** The pond target is a description of the relationship between the business of the corporation and the data inside the pond.
- **Pond data.** The data in the pond is merely the physical data that resides inside the pond.
- **Pond metadata.** The metadata describes the physical characteristics of the data contained in the data pond.
- **Pond metaprocess.** Metaprocess information is information about the transformation / conditioning of the data inside the data pond. In order to be useful, data in the pond must undergo a transformation / conditioning process.
- **Pond transformation criteria.** Pond transformation criteria are documentation of how the transformation / conditioning of data inside the pond should occur.

POND DESCRIPTOR

The pond descriptor has information such as:

- **Frequency of update or refreshment.** The update frequency or refreshment refers to the cycle with which data is sent to the data pond and/or the frequency or refreshment cycle of data outside the pond. This can be a regularly scheduled movement of data or update / refreshment can be on an as needed basis.

- **Source description.** The source description describes the lineage of the data in the data pond. In many cases, the lineage of data will pass through more than one source. This lineage information is useful to the analyst in determining the fitness of data in the data pond for analysis.

- **Volume of data.** The volume of data is a general description of how much data is in the data pond. Data is measured both in terms of number of records and in number of bytes. The volume of data greatly influences the type and depth of analysis that can be done.

- **Selection criteria.** The selection criteria are a description of the criteria that were used to select the data for inclusion in the data pond. The selection criteria of data are important to the analyst in determining what data is in the pond and why it is there.

- **Summarization criteria.** Most of the time, data is summarized or otherwise processed as it passes into the data pond. The summarization is a description of the algorithms employed. In some cases, data is transformed in a different model than summarization. This is a description of the algorithmic processing used in the shaping of the data in the data pond. The summarization criteria are useful to the analyst in determining how to do analysis.

- **Organization criteria.** Once the data is placed in the data pond, it is usually organized along the lines of the target of the pond. The target of the pond is similar to the data model of the business. The organization of data can be rigorous or casual, but in any case there is a description of exactly how the pond is organized. The description of the data organization is useful to the business analyst trying to make sense of the data pond.

- **Data relationships.** There normally are many data relationships among the data found in the pond. This is a description of those relationships. The data relationships are useful to the business analyst when it comes time to do business analysis.

POND TARGET

The pond target is the basic model that is used to shape the data in the data pond. The pond target can be as formal as a data model or can be as informal as a general description of the data found in the data pond. Typical pond target elements include such things as customer profile, sales record, shipment record, patient record, part number, inventory, SKU, telephone call record, click stream activity, delivery information, insurance claim, professor name, class name, class schedule, flight schedule, flight manifest, passenger record, reservation record, and so forth.

The pond target is the means by which a business relationship is made to the data in the data pond. The pond target is invaluable to the business analyst in planning how to conduct an analysis. There will then be, of necessity, a business relationship between the elements found in the target and the business itself.

POND DATA

The pond data is the physical manifestation of the data itself as it resides in the pond. The data can be organized in many ways depending on the storage mechanism for the data pond. In the world of Big Data, it is customary for the information to be stored in a "schema on read" manner. In this system, the data is initially stored in a block of data. Then when a query is made against the data, the system goes and reads the block of data and determines the schema inside the block.

By organizing data in this manner, very large amounts of data can be stored efficiently. However, by storing the data in a "schema on read" manner, the retrieval and analysis of the data can cause significant overhead for the system to bear. Every time data is accessed, *all* the data in the pond must be accessed in a "schema on read" organization of data.

POND METADATA

An important component of the data pond is the metadata that describes the physical characteristics of the data residing in the pond. The metadata is dependent on the data that exists outside the pond and the physical organization of the pond itself. If the data is stored in a standard DBMS outside the pond, many (or all) of those characteristics will be carried inside. In this case, the analyst can expect to find the same records, attributes, keys, and indexes.

But if the data is stored in document form outside the data pond, then the analyst can expect to find the data organized in a document by document organization. Even in the case of data stored in a "schema on read" system, metadata is still needed. However the data is physically organized inside the pond, it will be described by metadata. Without the metadata descriptions, the analyst would have a hard time figuring how to read and analyze the data pond. Fig 5.1 shows that metadata about the data in the data pond is contained inside the data pond itself.

Pond metadata

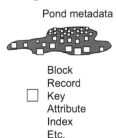

Block
Record
Key
Attribute
Index
Etc.

Fig 5.1 Storing the metadata about the data in the data pond

POND METAPROCESS

The metaprocess description of the transformation that takes place inside the data pond is found in the pond itself. Data enters the data pond in a raw state. Data is then "conditioned" or transformed into a form and structure that makes the data useful and intelligible to the analyst.

It is noteworthy that the conditioning process for each data pond is quite different than the conditioning process for other data ponds. The analog pond has its conditioning process which is quite different than the conditioning process for the application data pond or the textual data pond.

Metaprocess information may describe processing that has occurred outside the data pond as well. On occasion, significant business processing has occurred long before the data arrives at the data pond. It is entirely possible that metaprocess information can be gathered and stored when processing data. The metaprocess information describes the conditioning process that is necessary for each data pond, as seen in Fig 5.2.

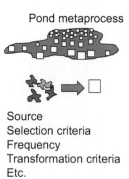

Pond metaprocess

Source
Selection criteria
Frequency
Transformation criteria
Etc.

Fig 5.2 Performing the conditioning processing for each data pond

POND TRANSFORMATION CRITERIA

The transformation criteria are a description of the criteria used in the transformation process for the conditioning of data within the data pond. Each of the data ponds has their own unique transformation criteria. The analog data pond may have a statement of the threshold for measurements. There may be a criterion that says: "If the length is greater than 45 cm then capture the record, else do not capture the record." Or there may be criterion that says: "Catch all measurements of a certain machine for the month of May."

In the application data pond, there might be criteria that looks like: "If gender = 0 then convert gender to female. If gender = 1 then convert gender to male. If gender = x then convert gender to female. If gender = y then convert gender to male, and so forth." Or there might be criteria that says: "If measurement is made in inches, then convert to centimeters."

In the textual data pond, there might be transformation criteria such as: "If word = Honda then add car to classification. If word = Porsche then add car to classification. If word = Ford then add car to classification. If word = Volkswagen, then add car to classification." Or there might be criterion that says: "If word = elm then type = tree. If word = oleander, then type = bush."

The transformation criteria is where the analyst goes to determine exactly how transformations have been accomplished. Fig 5.3 depicts the transformation criteria for each data pond.

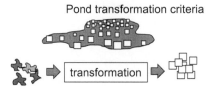

Fig 5.3 Determining the transformation criteria for each data pond

IN SUMMARY

Each data pond contains the following types of data:

- Pond descriptor
- Pond target
- Pond data
- Pond metadata
- Pond metaprocess
- Pond transformation criteria

Chapter 6
Analog Data Pond

The analog data pond is the place where data that begins life as a mechanically generated measurement of data resides. There are many sources for analog data – electronic eyes, manufacturing control machines, log or journal tapes, periodic metering measurements and so forth.

Analog data is often referred to as data measured by the "inch" or by the "millisecond." Inches and milliseconds refers to the frequency of measurement. Some products are laid out linearly and a snapshot is taken every n inches. Or a product is produced and is measured every millisecond. It does not take a fertile imagination to see that many, many irrelevant data points can result from a mechanical recording of measurements.

ANALOG DATA ISSUES

There are two generic issues with the data in the analog data pond. The first is the sheer volume of data. It is normal for there to be a massive amount of data that is generated by analog processing. A machine just sits there and takes a snapshot every millisecond. It is also normal for 99.9% of the data to be normal and of little business value. The same (or nearly same) value is repeated over and over. In a sense, the interesting data "hides" behind the tremendous volume of information generated.

A second issue is that much of the important data associated with the generation of the analog data is lost. Analog analysts have the habit of collecting only the analog data and not the descriptor data that is associated with the analog data. Unfortunately, the descriptor data is often as valuable (or even more valuable) than the actual analog data.

The challenge the analyst has in dealing with analog data is in preparing the data for analysis by streamlining and outlining the important analog data. This streamlining and outlining is accomplished in the transformation / conditioning process that occurs inside the analog data pond.

DATA DESCRIPTOR

The details surrounding the information in the analog data pond is very important. Some of the surrounding data includes:

- The selection criteria for the data that finds its way into the analog data pond

- The originating source of the analog data

- The frequency with which analog data is moved into the analog data pond

- The volume of analog data that is moved into the analog data pond

- The date and time that the movement of analog occurs.

Fig 6.1 depicts the analog data pond.

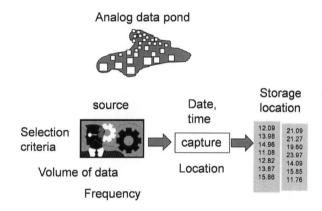

Fig 6.1 Storing data in the analog data pond

CAPTURING RAW DATA/TRANSFORMING RAW DATA

There are two basic steps that occur as analog data is moved into the analog data pond. The first step is capturing and moving the analog data into the data pond. The second step is the transformation / conditioning of the analog data in the analog data pond into a form and structure that is easily analyzed by the end user.

Note that the activity of transformation of the analog data occurs entirely within the confines of the analog data pond itself.

Fig 6.2 shows the capture and transformation activities.

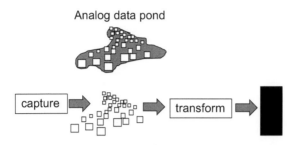

Fig 6.2 Capturing and transforming activities in the analog data pond

TRANSFORMING/CONDITIONING RAW ANALOG DATA

The most interesting aspect of the analog data pond is conditioning the raw analog data into a form that is useful for analysis. The process of conditioning can be called a transformation or a conversion.

In an earlier day and age, the process of conversion was called data reduction and/or data compression. The purpose of data reduction was to significantly reduce the amount of storage and the number of records that was required. And significantly reducing the amount of storage required for data reduces the amount of work required by the system to do analytical processing of the data.

The data reduction found in the analog data pond is entirely up to the analyst managing the data. The type and amount of data reduction will vary from one set to another.

Some of the techniques of data reduction that can be employed are:

- **Deduplication**. Deduplication entails the removal of masses of redundant data.

- **Excision**. Data excision calls for the removal of unneeded data and data that is unlikely to ever be needed for analysis.

- **Compression**. Data compression allows data to be packed very tightly. The problem with compression arises when compressed data must be altered. It is difficult to alter highly compressed data without incurring a high overhead.

- **Smoothing**. Smoothing of data is the practice of removing or editing outliers.

- **Interpolation**. Interpolation of data is the practice of inferring values of data based on the values near to the value being created. The interpolated value is the "likely" value, had a value been found.

- **Sampling**. The practice of sampling data is the practice of selecting a small subset of data that is representative of a larger set of data. Sampling is good for analytical processing but cannot be used for detailed update processing.

- **Rounding**. Rounding is the processing of removing and rounding insignificant digits from a data set.

- **Encoding**. Encoding is the practice of representing long strings of data with shorter strings of data.

- **Tokenization**. Tokenization is a form of encoding. Tokenization can be used effectively when there is a high degree of repetition in the data being stored.

- **Threshholding.** Threshholding is a form of excision. In threshholding only values above (or below) the threshold are stored. Everything within the boundaries of the threshold are ignored.

- **Clustering.** Clustering of data is the practice of grouping similar and exact values of data. Clustering is a form of data deduplication.

And there are many other forms of data reduction.

One or more of these techniques can be used for any given set of analog data inside the analog data pond. Fig 6.3 shows that a fundamental transformation of data occurs from the time the data enters the analog data pond to the time that data is fit for analysis.

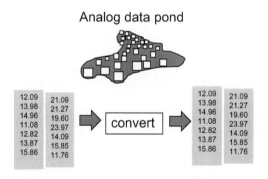

Fig 6.3 Making the data useful for analysis in the data pond

Some of the common forms of data reduction inside the analog data pond will be discussed in the following sections.

Data Excision

Perhaps the most common and useful form of data reduction is data excision. In data excision, data that is not needed is simply removed. So how does the analyst tell that data is not needed? There are lots of ways. One of these is rounding. Suppose a measurement is made saying that a wheel is 16.577638892 cm in diameter. In practice, the only digits that are significant are the first two following the decimal point. As a consequence, rounding up to the first two digits makes sense. The number 16.577638892 is rounded up to 16.58, thereby saving significant space.

Another form of excision is that of threshholding. Suppose a manufacturing process is being tracked. The output is measured by an electronic eye. As long as the part is no longer than 1.257 cm and is no shorter than 1.250 cm, then the part is in compliance. The electronic eye reads the following parts as they come off the assembly line:

```
1.256937
1.251004
1.249887
1.254887
1.261095
1.255087
1.252090
1.254981
```

Using the boundaries of threshholding, the system would record only the data that was not in the boundaries of tolerance. In this case, the system would record the values 1.249887 and 1.261095. The other values are in the threshold of tolerance found by the system. Fig 6.4 shows that excision of data is a useful tool for data reduction.

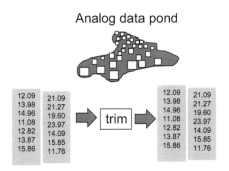

Analog data pond

Fig 6.4 Excising data in the analog data pond

CLUSTERING DATA

Another useful technique is that of clustering data. There are different forms of clustering data. One of those forms is that of grouping common values or ranges of values. Suppose there were the following measurements:

```
1.56
1.78
1.67
1.57
1.65
1.70
1.62
1.73
1.77
```

A more concise way to represent the data is to cluster them. The clustering might look like:

```
1.5 - 2
1.6 - 3
1.7 - 4
```

In this clustering, there are 2 values from 1.50 to 1.59, 3 values from 1.60 to 1.69 and 4 values from 1.70 to 1.79.

Another way to cluster the data is:

```
1.5 (1), (4)
1.6 (3), (5), (7)
1.7 (2), (6),(8),(9)
```

In this method, the ordinal number is maintained. Note that in the first method of clustering the ordinal number of the value is lost.

But in either case, there is the potential for gross reduction of the amount of space required to represent the numbers. And in fact, there are many more complicated forms of clustering, like bit map indexing. Fig 6.5 depicts clustering as a form of data reduction that can be useful in conditioning data in the analog data pond.

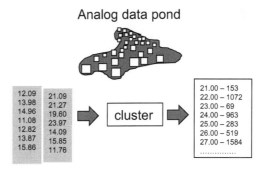

Fig 6.5 Clustering data in the analog data pond

DATA RELATIONSHIPS

Another form of data conditioning that can be useful in the analog data pond is that of establishing relationships between measurements of data. As an example, suppose we measured air pressure for tires and those measurements were captured as:

```
35.6 psi
36.1 psi
34.6 psi
36.2 psi
34.8 psi
35.7 psi
35.9 psi
```

While the tire pressure may be an interesting number, the measurement becomes more interesting when the tire manufacturer is attached to the pressure. Consider what the attachment of manufacturer looks like:

```
35.6 psi Goodrich
36.1 psi Bridgestone
34.6 psi Goodyear
36.2 psi Bridgestone
34.8 psi Alliance
35.7 psi Michelin
35.9 psi Panther
```

Once the tire manufacturer is attached to the pressure, more possibilities for analysis arise. But suppose even more data were available. If the date the tire was installed were attached to the data, the results might look like:

```
35.6 psi Goodrich July 20, 2016
36.1 psi Bridgestone Jan 5, 2013
34.6 psi Goodyear Oct 6, 2015
36.2 psi Bridgestone Nov 17, 2016
34.8 psi Alliance Dec 20, 2015
35.7 psi Michelin Mar 2, 2013
35.9 psi Panther Apr 28, 2014
```

And there are even more types of data that could be added. For example, suppose the mileage the tire had on it was added to the data. The result might look like:

```
35.6 psi Goodrich July 20, 2016 16,500 miles
36.1 psi Bridgestone Jan 5, 2013 85,980 miles
34.6 psi Goodyear Oct 6, 2015 24,000 miles
36.2 psi Bridgestone Nov 17, 2016 2,000 miles
34.8 psi Alliance Dec 20, 2015 14,970 miles
35.7 psi Michelin Mar 2, 2013 78,400 miles
35.9 psi Panther Apr 28, 2014 65,980 miles
```

Fig 6.6 shows that adding relationships to data in the analog data pond greatly enhances the usability and desirability of data.

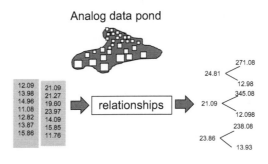

Fig 6.6 Making the analog data pond more valuable through relationships

PROBABILITY OF FUTURE USAGE

All the design decisions shaping the transformation and conditioning of the data in the analog data pond are shaped by probability of future usage. If a unit of data has a very low probability of future access or even no probability of access, then it can safely be removed from the analog data pond. But if a unit of data has a high probability of access, then it is moved to a prominent place in the analog data pond. In fact the higher the probability of access the more prominently the data is placed in the analog data pond.

Of course not all probabilities can be accurately predicted. Because of this fact of life, it often makes sense to not throw away data that has a low probability of access, but to place that data in a less conspicuous location.

Fig 6.7 shows that probability of future access to data shapes all design decisions of the conditioning and transformation structure of the analog data pond.

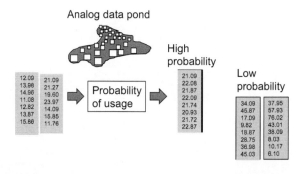

Fig 6.7 Determining the probability of usage in the analog data pond

OUTLIERS

Another factor of data in the analog data pond that sparks interest among the analyst is the occurrence of outliers. An outlier is the measurement of an event occurrence that does not fit the norm. Typically, the measurements have a pattern. There are often small variations from the pattern but most of the measurements fit a predictable and definable pattern. An outlier is a measurement that does not fit the pattern of the other variables nor has a variance which is atypical of the other variables. Fig 6.8 shows a collection of measurements of data and a few outliers.

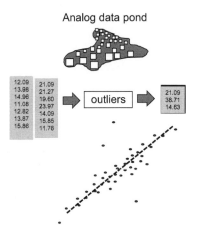

Fig 6.8 Capturing outliers in the analog data pond

Outliers are always of interest and typically deserve special study. As an example of outliers, suppose a telephone company does an analysis of the length of calls made from New Jersey to Texas. Most of the phone calls last five to six minutes. Some phone calls are shorter and some phone calls are longer, but most are in that range. However, the telephone company notices that there are three calls greater than 24 hours.

The phone company decides to investigate those really long calls and finds that:

- One call was a computer working with another computer transferring data.

- One call was a malfunction of the equipment. The call actually only lasted a minute but the monitoring equipment had a problem and the call appeared to be a really long call.

- The last call was a customer who was downloading movies and was mistakenly using the wrong line to make the download.

When the organization examines the outliers, it can then decide what it wants to do with them. One option is to remove them from the data set. Another option is to redefine the data set to include them. A third option is to create another data set with a new algorithm defining the distribution of the measurements.

Once the data has been conditioned, it is then made available to the analyst. The analyst then uses the transformed/conditioned data for the purpose of analysis, as seen in Fig 6.9.

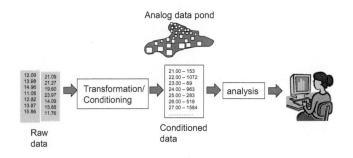

Fig 6.9 Analyzing data in the analog data pond

SPECIALIZED AD HOC ANALYSIS

There is another use for the analog data that has been conditioned. It is entirely possible and likely that specialized analysis needs to be done. It is also possible to use the conditioned data as a basis for a specialized data analysis.

Say the conditioned data is for a manufacturing environment. Analog analysis regularly uses the conditioned data for their analysis. But suppose a new manufacturer arrives in the marketplace. The corporation wishes to do a separate analysis of a subset of the products that they produce. There is nothing wrong with separating out the specialized product from the mainstream products and performing a specialized analysis. With the conditioned data, it is an easy task to use it as a foundation on which to do new and unanticipated analysis. Fig 6.10 depicts the fact that ad hoc specialized analysis can be done from the conditioned data.

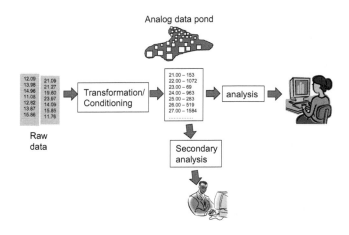

Fig 6.10 Performing ad hoc specialized analysis in the analog data pond

IN SUMMARY

The analog data pond then is the place where analog data is stored, conditioned and analyzed. The conditioning process varies for every type of data found in the analog data pond. Fig 6.11 shows the analog data pond.

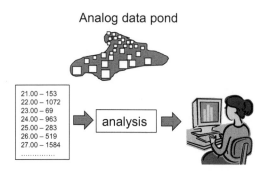

Fig 6.11 Analyzing data in the analog data pond

Chapter 7
Application Data Pond

The application data pond is where application related data is placed. Much of (but not all) application data is transaction related. A transaction occurs and an electronic record is made of the transaction. The electronic record is stored and used in the operational systems of the corporation. The electronic record is then used to conduct current business. After the electronic record has fulfilled its active life in the operational environment, the record of the transaction finds its way into the application data pond.

Another form of operational application data may find its way into the application data pond. There may be customer lists, product catalogs, packing lists, shipment schedules, delivery schedules, phone call records, and so forth that are all captured as operational application data.

DNA OF DATA

One of the shaping factors in application data is the infrastructure of the operational system. The original recording of the data as it is captured and settles into the operational application has a profound effect on the storage and organization of the data that arrives in the application data bank. In many ways the original operational application capturing and storing the data becomes the

DNA of the application data. The DNA of the application data is as profound as the ethnic race that each person on Earth has in his/her background. In one form or another, each person has their own ethnic origin, and the DNA of the person affects that person all their life. It affects their health, their height and weight, and many other aspects of life. DNA is one of the defining characteristics of application data, just as it is with life.

Operational application data has the same profound DNA origins. The operational processing of data determines the level of data granularity, data organization, contents of the data, the business events which are noteworthy, the timing of the events, the way data is shaped and stored, and so forth. Fig 7.1 shows that the application infrastructure has a profound influence on data as it enters the application data pond.

Application data pond

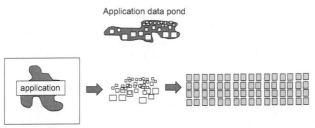

Fig 7.1 Influencing the data as it arrives in the data pond

DESCRIPTORS

The descriptors of the application data include such items as the source of the application data, the approximate volume of the application data, the frequency with which the application data is harvested, and other related information.

The descriptor information is useful to the analyst in the application data pond in determining how to create and accurately analyze application data.

It's normal for the application data pond to contain data from many applications. For a large corporation that is almost always true. It's also possible but quite rare that all of the application data that resides in the data pond come from a single application of data. Nearly all large corporations run on a multiplicity of applications, both in-house and vendor solutions. Fig 7.2 depicts the descriptors of the application data pond.

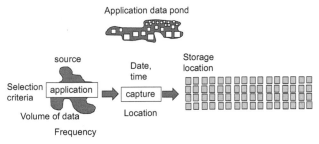

Fig 7.2 Depicting the descriptors of the application data pond

STANDARD DATABASE FORMAT

It is normal for application-based data to be entered into the application data pond in a standard relational database format. Most applications have data stored in a row and column format. So application data will usually be stored and transported into the application data pond in this standard database format.

Note that this assumption about the application data pond is very different than the assumptions made about the analog data pond. In the analog data pond, information arrives in a raw data state – usually a long list of measurements. In the application data pond, it is common for the data to arrive in a database format.

Interestingly, just because data arrives into the application data pond in a database format does not mean the advantages of a database are necessarily carried with the application data. Just because data was created in a relational database format does not mean the discipline and rigor that accompany a database will extend to the application data pond. Once the application data is in the data pond, it is governed by whatever technology is used to manage the application data pond, which most likely is not a standard database management system.

BASIC ORGANIZATION OF DATA

Because of the application origin of the data, details in the application data pond typically are divided into records. Records have attributes and some attributes can be keys, while other attributes can be indexed. Fig 7.3 shows the basic organization of data inside the application data pond.

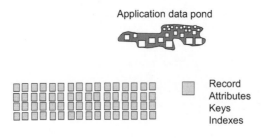

Application data pond

Record
Attributes
Keys
Indexes

Fig 7.3 Organizing data inside the application data pond

INTEGRATION OF DATA

When data arrives in the application data pond, it may or may not have a business related structure. If the data has been integrated before being passed to the application data pond, then it may have a structure inherently embedded into the data. But if the data has not been integrated along the lines of business before entering the application data pond, then the data will not magically become integrated.

Having an integrated business orientation means the data is organized along the lines of the major subject areas of the organization. Typical corporate subjects are customer, product, shipment, order, delivery, and so forth.

It is mandatory that the data have an integrated alignment with the business if the analyst is to make any sense of the data. The biggest impediment to the effective analysis of data in the application data pond is the lack of integration.

DATA MODEL

In order to achieve integration of the data in the application data pond, it is necessary to have a data model in place. Usually there is a corporate data model. If there is no corporate data model, then there are generic business models which are available.

Care must be taken in selecting the data model for the application data pond. Separate data models are needed for business operations than warehouse operations, for example. In most cases, the corporate data warehouse data model is the appropriate model for the application data pond. Fig 7.4 shows the data model which becomes the "target" for the application data pond.

Application data pond

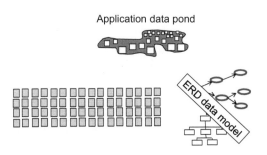

Fig 7.4 Creating the data model "target" of the application data pond

There are many advantages to the data model. One advantage is that the data model provides high-level guidance as to how data should be related. This high-level perspective is through entities and relationships or subject areas. But there is a lower level perspective that accompanies the data model. At the more detailed level, the data model provides a guide to such important elements as metadata. The metadata gives a detailed description of the data, such as defining records and their meaning, attributes and their meaning, keys, indexes, data relationships and so forth.

The analyst preparing to use the application data pond finds the metadata definitions very useful in preparing an analysis of the data in the application data pond. But the data model for the application pond has one complication that classical data models do not have. The application data pond holds data over a lengthy period of time, but the data model itself changes over time. As a result, the data model for the application data pond needs to be quite flexible.

The analyst needs to know what changes have been made to metadata over time, since they have to be factored in to the analysis of the data found in the application data pond. So the data model for the application data pond is a very sophisticated model.

NECESSITY OF INTEGRATION

If data finds its way into the application data pond in an integrated state, the organization is lucky. If data finds its way into the application data pond in an unintegrated state (which is the normal case) the organization must transform the data after it has entered the application data pond. This transformation step is very similar to conditioning for the analog data pond.

If data is to be meaningfully used for analysis in the application data pond, the transformation of data into an integrated state is absolutely necessary. There are many reasons for the transformation and integration of application data pond data. Consider the following set of transformations, as seen in Fig 7.5.

The different applications have gender encoding. In order to make the analysis consistent, the application data needs to be transformed into a consistent definition of gender. The same considerations hold true for measurement of distance. Inches and feet and yards need to be converted to centimeters if consistent and meaningful analysis is to be done.

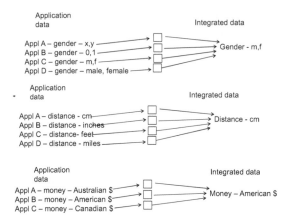

Fig 7.5 Transforming data in the application data pond

The same sort of conversion must be done to put Australian and Canadian dollars in a consistent currency, for example.

Unfortunately the conversions for integration that need to be made in the figure are only the tip of the iceberg. There are *many, many* other conversions required in order to transform the data into an integrated state. And the analyst cannot do meaningful analysis unless the data has been converted. Fig 7.6 shows that a fundamental transformation of data is needed within the application data pond from the time data enters until such time as data is usable within the pond.

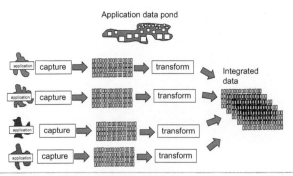

Fig 7.6 Transforming until the data is useable

POINTING FROM ONE APPLICATION TO THE NEXT

In some cases when two applications are merged, the result is a pointer from one to the next. This is a simple relationship.

As an example, consider the business activity of placing an order for tickets for a Saturday night performance. There is a customer application, database, and ticket order application with database. In this case, there might be a simple structuring of the customer application that looks like:

```
Bill Inmon
John Williams
Carol Renne
Georgia Burleson
Jeanne Friedman
```

The ticket database might look like:

```
Sat night 7:15 seat A12
Sat night 7:15 seat A13
Sat night 7:15 seat A14
Sat night 7:15 seat A16
```

Once the data is integrated, the result might look like:

```
Bill Inmon Seat A12, seat A13
John Williams
Carol Renne Seat A15
Georgia Burleson Seat A14
Jeanne Friedman
```

Fig 7.7 shows the integration of a simple pointer relationship between applications.

Application data pond

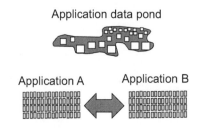

Application A   Application B

Fig 7.7 Integrating data within the application data pond

INTERSECTING APPLICATIONS

A more complex relationship is that of two applications intersecting. When two applications have an intersection there is data independently created as a result of the crossover. The independently created data forms its own independent collection of data. As an example of an independently created collection of application data, suppose there was an oil company and a gasoline distribution company. On Sept 2, the distribution company makes a delivery of gasoline. The database might look like:

```
Oil Company Distribution Company
Standard Oil Flying Horse Shipping
Conoco Akers Distributing
Texaco
```

Now suppose a set of deliveries were done. A delivery might look like:

```
Delivery AS15-YR
From Standard Oil
To 6534 Wolfensberger Road
Castle Rock, CO
By Flying Horse Shipping
Amount: 2000 gallons
Date Sept 2
```

The intersecting data stands in compliance with the existing application data. Fig 7.8 shows that there can be intersection data in the application data pond as well as other types of data.

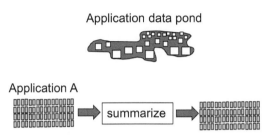

Fig 7.8 Different types of data in the application data pond

SUBSETS OF DATA IN THE APPLICATION DATA POND

On occasion, the analyst may wish to select data from application data that have already been integrated. This too is a possibility. Fig 7.9 shows that a subset of data from an application can be selected and stored in the application data pond.

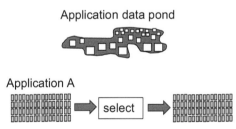

Fig 7.9 Choosing an application subset to store in the application data pond

As an example of data that can be selected, suppose the application database contains all telephone calls made in the month of May. The analyst may wish to select all phone calls greater than three minutes made on May 15. In doing so, the analyst greatly narrows down the work the system has to do in order to find the data they are looking for.

IN SUMMARY

Once data has been integrated, it is now fit for analysis. Fig 7.10 shows that analysis can be done on data in an integrated application data pond.

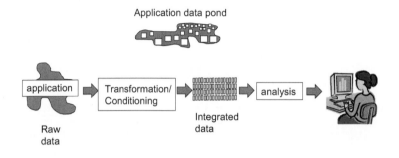

Fig 7.10 Analyzing data in the application data pond

The DNA of an application is the infrastructure of the data as it exists in the operational environment. The infrastructure of operational data extends well into the application data pond. The data descriptors found in the application data pond are of great use to the analyst.

The normal case is for data in the operational environment to have been stored in a relational format. The relational format has records, attributes, keys, indexes and so forth. When the data is placed in an application data pond, the data reflects its relational origins even though the data management of the application data pond is not a relational DBMS.

However it occurs, data in the application data pond must be integrated. Integration is a necessity of the business analyst that will be using the data.

Data in the application data pond goes through a conditioning process, just as data in the analog data pond must be conditioned. However, the conditioning that occurs in the application data pond is very different from the conditioning that occurs in the analog data pond.

Chapter 8
Textual Data Pond

The third kind of data collection is the textual data pond. There is much textual data in the corporate world. Unfortunately, very little textual data is ever converted to a state where it's fit for analysis or is ever used as a basis for decision making. Yet there is a tremendous amount of textual information that has a lot of potential. There is no reason why textual data that finds its way to the textual data pond cannot be used for analytical processing.

UNIFORM DATA AND THE COMPUTER

The reason why textual data has such a hard time being used for corporate decision making is that the computer requires data to be served up in a uniform manner. The computer is good at reading one record, processing it, then reading another record that was in the same format as the previous record. The system thrives on repetition of processing. When the computer has to change its mindset with every record, it will have a hard time. And with text, every word must be treated as a completely new universe.

For this reason, text has been treated in a very superficial manner within the bounds of computerized processing. Computer technology and text (i.e., narration) are the digital equivalent of oil and water. They just don't mix well.

VALUABLE TEXT

Some of the many places where text contains valuable information for making managerial decisions include:

- Corporate contracts
- Corporate call center conversations
- Customer feedback
- Medical records
- Insurance claims
- Human resource records
- Insurance policies
- Loans applications
- Corporate memos
- And many other places.

However, most corporations collect their text, put it in a file, and never look at or analyze it again. The info just sits in a file and collects dust.

There is a good reason why corporation don't look at text: there's so much of it. If a person were to sit down and read a large collection of text, the person would not be able to recall a small fraction of what was read. The human brain is just not a good processor of large amounts of textual data.

TEXTUAL DISAMBIGUATION

A profound technology called "textual disambiguation" has changed the ability of text to be used for decision making. That technology is used for reading and analyzing text and then transforming text into a standard database format, with the context of the text identified in the database format.

Most corporations have not yet discovered textual disambiguation. That's why most text arrives in the textual data pond in a state of raw text. Sometimes text arrives as formal language, informal notes, slang, vulgarities or even other languages.

The most common text forms are emails, tweets and other social media, but the data can also arrive via physical reading technology such as OCR (optical character recognition) or voice transcription. However it arrives at the textual data pond, documents and text are usually still in the form of unstructured (to a computer) narration.

TEXT SENT TO THE DATA POND

Fig 8.1 shows documents that have been captured and have been sent to the textual data pond.

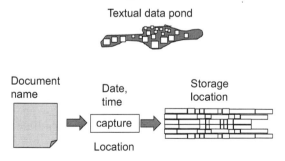

Fig 8.1 Sending documents to the textual data pond

If the corporation attempts to read and make sense of the text in its raw, narrative state, they'll find that only a very superficial analysis can be done. If the corporation is serious about making use of the textual data pond, it is mandatory to pass the raw text through textual disambiguation.

Note that textual disambiguation is merely another form of transforming and conditioning data. The need to condition and transform data is seen in both the analog data pond and the application data pond. However, textual disambiguation is very different from data reduction or integration of application data.

So it is not unusual that textual data in the pond needs to go through its own conditioning and transformation process. What is noteworthy is that the different processes used for conditioning and transforming the data ponds are completely different from each other. There is very, very little overlap (if any) among the different techniques used to condition and transform data in the different data ponds. Fig 8.2 shows the need for textual disambiguation in the textual data pond.

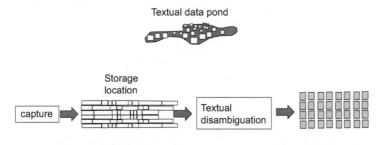

Textual data pond

Storage location

capture

Textual disambiguation

Fig 8.2 Applying textual disambiguation in the textual data pond

OUTPUT OF TEXTUAL DISAMBIGUATION

The net effect of textual disambiguation is the ability to store text in a standard, uniformly structured database and to store the text along with its context. Once text is restructured into that format, the text can be read and analyzed by standard analytical processors.

In order to store the text in a standard database format, it is necessary to store the text in a form where there is a record. Each record has the text that is processed, along with its context, the byte number of the text, and the name of the document. In order to visualize how this might look, consider the following example in Fig 8.3.

Text

Housing Lease 026-B1
This lease is assigned to Bill Inmon, resident at 256 Lyons Court, Castle Rock, CO 80104. The above named resident has made this lease from Jan 1, 2005 to Dec 31, 2009 for the Sum of $4,000 payable upon completion of this document. The above named resident agrees to allow inspection from time to time by the leaseholder – Akron Lease Company.
....

Disambiguated Data base

Doc-id, byte, text, context

026-B1, 5, lease, leasehold
026-B1, 28, Bill Inmon, leaseholder
026-B1, 37, 256 Lyons Court, address
026-B1, 56, 80104, zip code
026-B1, 98, Jan 1, 2005, startdate
....

Fig 8.3 Disambiguating text example

Here, a lease has been made between an individual and a corporation. The text defines the terms of the lease. The lease has been read and passed through textual disambiguation. Once having been processed, the text has been reduced to a database format. In the database format are the identification of the document, the byte address of the text that has been captured, the text itself, and the context of the text.

Once the text has been reduced to the form of a database and once the context of the text has been determined, the text can then be read by a computer and processed analytically. It is interesting to examine the functions that textual disambiguation performs in the act of disambiguating text.

INHERENT COMPLEXITY

Language is inherently complex so it is no surprise that textual disambiguation is quite complex as well. Indeed, there are over 90 different functions that algorithmically define the inner workings of textual disambiguation. Some of (but not all of!) the more interesting workings of textual disambiguation will be described here:

- **Inline contextualization.** Inline contextualization is the process of identifying text and its context by examining the words that surround it. For example, given the text ...signed by Bill Inmon, leaseholder... Inline contextualization only works on text that has predictable occurrences of data such as a contract. In this case, the leaseholder is identified as "Bill Inmon."

- **Proximity.** Words in proximity to each other have different meanings than words not in proximity to each other. Given the text ...Denver Broncos won the Super Bowl... the words Denver Broncos are taken to mean a professional football team. Proximity analysis works on words in any order.

- **Alternate spelling.** In England, the word color is spelled colour. Alternate spelling analysis works for many types of functions.

- **Homographic resolution.** In many cases the interpretation of a word or acronym is shaped by the understanding of who wrote the term. A cardiologist interprets "ha" as heart attack. An endocrinologist interprets "ha" as hepatitis A, while a general practitioner interprets "ha" as head ache, and so forth. Homographic resolution is a sophisticated form of alternate spelling.

- **Acronym resolution.** In the military, AWOL means absent without leave. Acronym resolution is a form of alternate spelling.

- **Custom variable recognition.** In the US, the digits 999 999 9999 are interpreted to mean a telephone number. Corporations have *many* variables which are recognizable by the structure of the variable itself.

- **Taxonomy resolution.** When a document refers to a Volkswagen or a Honda, it is referring to a car. Taxonomy resolution is the single most important function of textual disambiguation.

- **Date standardization.** July 5, 1999 is the same thing as 1999/07/05. Date standardization is very common and is very useful.

This short list of functions merely reflects some of the more prominent functions of textual disambiguation. There are many more functions that need to be accomplished by textual disambiguation in order for text to be reduced to the form of a database.

It is noteworthy that merely processing text is not enough to do analytic processing. In order to do effective analytic processing, it is necessary to identify and to process context as well. And context of text is much more difficult to handle than the text itself.

TEXTUAL DISAMBIGUATION FUNCTIONALITY

Fig 8.4 shows some of the functions of textual disambiguation.

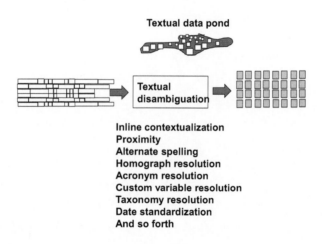

Fig 8.4 Disambiguating text functions

TAXONOMIES AND ONTOLOGIES

Each data pond has a target that allows the data in the pond to relate to the business of the organization. In the application data pond, there was the corporate data model. But the corporate data model does not relate well to the world of text. Instead, in text there are taxonomies and ontologies.

Taxonomies are classifications of terms. There are many, many taxonomies in the world. As some simple examples of a taxonomy, consider the following:

```
Car
  Honda
  Porsche
  Volkswagen
  Ford
  Toyota
Or
Tree
  Elm
  Pine
  Fir
  Oak
  Walnut
```

A taxonomy then is nothing but a classification of terms. An ontology is a grouping of related taxonomies. For another example of an ontology, consider the following:

```
Country
  USA
  Canada
  Mexico
  Australia
  South Africa
And
USA
  Texas
  New Mexico
  Arizona
  Colorado
```

The relationship between taxonomies is that the US is made up of states. Together these two taxonomies form an ontology.

There are an almost infinite number of taxonomies (and ontologies). Taxonomies and ontologies form the target foundation for the textual data pond as seen in Fig 8.5.

Textual data pond

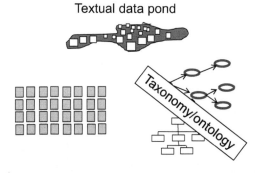

Fig 8.5 Leveraging taxonomies and ontologies in the textual data pond

VALUE OF TEXT AND CONTEXT

The value of having both text and context can be illustrated very easily. Suppose you have some text about people. You have different names in your text. You have Joe and you have Susan and you have Mike and you have Terry. Now suppose you want to find Joe who is an army officer. If you do a query against all Joe's, you get bartenders, convicts, newborn babies and airplane pilots. But if you have information about all Joe's that have been identified by context, say government employees, you can now make a query and find the Joe (or Joe's) that are army officers.

Context allows you to qualify exactly what you are looking for and to the business analyst, that is a necessary condition.

Fig 8.6 depicts the usage of context in a query format.

Analysis using text and context

Examine _text_ where context = _xxxxxxxxx_

Fig 8.6 Applying context in the textual data pond

In this case a query would be made that says:

Find all occurrences of "Joe" where context = army officer.

The results of the query would be a reference to all people named Joe who are army officers.

TRACING TEXT BACK TO THE SOURCE

In case there was a question as to the validity or accuracy of the query, any reference to text can always be traced easily and quickly back to the originating source.

The reason why it is easy to trace a reference back to the originating source is that when textual disambiguation is done, the byte of the document and the name of the document are stored with each reference. Therefore, whenever you have a question about the work that has been done by textual disambiguation, you can always go back to the original document and verify that disambiguation was performed correctly.

MECHANICS OF DISAMBIGUATION

As an example of the mechanics of disambiguation, consider the taxonomy developed to identify sentiment. Sentiment occurs in many places – in tweets, in emails, in documents, and so forth. It is often quite useful to gauge tone in the message. The way tone is evaluated is through the usage of a sentiment taxonomy. Fig 8.7 shows a simple taxonomy that can be used to identify sentiment in text.

Classifying sentiment

Negative	Positive
dislike	liked
disagreed	loved
did not like	ate it up
unhappy	gobbled
upset	admired
hated	felt comfortable
horrible	cherished
terrible	feel good
ugly	....
....	

Fig 8.7 Applying sentiment analysis in the textual data pond

In reality, a sentiment taxonomy would be *much more* involved than that shown in the figure. The simple taxonomy above is merely for the purposes of illustration.

Textual disambiguation reads the raw text and then matches the contents of the taxonomy against the raw text that is being analyzed. When a word is discovered that matches a word in the taxonomy, the inference is made that the message has an expression of sentiment. In such a fashion, a document can be analyzed and the tone of the document gauged.

Once the tone of the document is weighted and placed into a database, then multiple messages can be analyzed by the computer using standard analytical and standard visualization technology.

ANALYZING THE DATABASE

By creating a database, the computer can then perform the heavy lifting analysis. As an example, suppose there was a restaurant chain receiving feedback from its customers. Many customers are sending messages on a daily basis.

The messages cover a wide spectrum of topics. Some discuss the menu. One item was too salty. Another too hot. Another item had too small of portions. Others discuss the waiter/waitress. The waiter was slow. The waiter had a bad attitude. The waitress was very nice. Some topics dealt with cleanliness. The floor was wet. The table was not wiped. The lights were too dim. Other topics were about almost anything you could imagine – the parking lot, the restroom, the vending machines, and so forth.

In a month's time, the restaurant chain receives over 100,000 messages from its customers. There simply are too many messages for any person to read and assimilate the information contained in the messages. Yet the feedback from the customer is critical to the happiness of the customer experience. And the happiness of the customer is the key to customer loyalty *and repeat business*. It greatly behooves the restaurant chain to listen to its customers.

So the restaurant chain decides to run its customer feedback through textual disambiguation. After reading 100,000 messages a month, a database is created. The database is then read into standard analytical software, which allows them to send canned, but still personalized automated responses.

VISUALIZING THE RESULTS

A visualization is produced that looks like that seen in Fig 8.8.

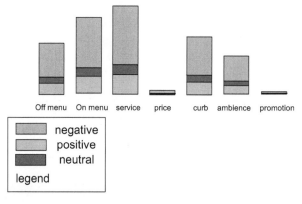

Fig 8.8 Visualizing feedback in the textual data pond

The different categories of comments are divided into several categories:

- Off menu items – non entrée items on the menu
- On menu items – the entrees served by the restaurant chain
- Service – comments about the waiters, waitresses, cashier, manager, etc.
- Price – the cost of food
- Curb – comments about the exterior of the restaurant and service outside the restaurant
- Ambience – how clean the restaurant is, what atmosphere the restaurant has
- Promotions – what comments there are about the promotions done by the restaurant.

A word of wisdom is needed to explain the interpretation of comment sentiment. At first glance it appears there are a lot of negative comments. But experience has shown that people are more inclined to message a restaurant when there is a negative experience. When a person goes to a restaurant and has a pleasant experience there is rarely feedback for the restaurant. Therefore a ratio of 85%:15% of negative to positive experiences is the normal expectation.

If a restaurant is getting more than 85% negative comments then something is wrong. If less than 85% negative, that branch is doing something right.

Looking at the comments and their sentiment expressed in Fig 8.9 shows some surprising results. One is that there are almost no comments at all about price. This is an indication to management that it may not be charging enough for its food. The same sort of observation can be made about promotions. There simply are no comments that anyone makes about the promotions the restaurant is doing. This implies that the promotions are ineffective. The message that the restaurant chain is not charging enough and that it ought to be doing more effective promotions is really important to the management of the chain.

In Summary

The textual data pond is the place where text resides. In order to be effective, text must go through a transformation and conditioning process. The transformation and conditioning process is called textual disambiguation.

The net result of textual disambiguation is the creation of text in a standard database format where both text and context have been identified. Fig 8.9 shows the textual data pond.

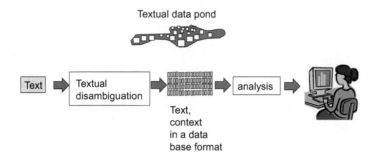

Fig 8.9 Analyzing text in the textual data pond

Chapter 9
Comparing the Ponds

At first glance, the different data ponds seem to be the same. While there are many structural similarities among the different ponds, there are some important and distinct structural dissimilarities as well.

SIMILARITIES ACROSS THE DATA PONDS

In terms of similarities, all data ponds:

- Ingest raw data, usually lots of it
- Transform/condition the raw data into a form that is suitable for analysis
- Produce a uniform, integrated structuring of data that is suitable for analytical processing
- Support business analysis with their final output
- Ultimately send their data to the archival data pond
- Have similar entry points for raw data
- Produce data that is fit for analytical processing
- Have a supporting infrastructure of documentation to help the business analyst.

From a structural standpoint then, there are many core similarities among the different ponds of data. But for all the structural similarities, there are some important and striking differences as well.

DISSIMILARITIES ACROSS THE DATA PONDS

The structural dissimilarities among the different data ponds include:

- The raw data entering the pond is very different from the raw data found in other ponds. One pond contains analog data, another pond contains application data, and another pond contains textual data.

- The transformation and conditioning process for each pond is very, very different from one pond to the next.

- The type of business analysis conducted on the final data state of the pond is very different.

RELATIONAL FORMAT FOR FINAL STATE DATA

An interesting question arises when looking at the different pools. Does the technology holding the final state of the pool have to be in a relational format? Fig 9.1 poses this question.

Is there anything sacred about the final
form of output being in a relational format?

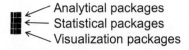

Analytical packages
Statistical packages
Visualization packages

Fig 9.1 Requiring a relational format?

The answer is no. There is nothing special about the relational format other than the fact that the vast majority of analytical and visualization packages available operate against relational data. The world of analytical processing has been around for a long time, long before there were data ponds. It is no surprise that analytical processing supports the relational data model.

Having stated that, there is no other reason why the final state data in the data pond must be in a relational format. If there is an analytical tool that operates on data in other than a relational format, then there is no reason why that analytical package cannot be used.

TECHNOLOGY DIFFERENCES

A related question is whether the final data state of each pond has to be in the same technology. The only reason why an organization might want the technology to be the same is because of the overhead of supporting more than one platform.

TOTAL EXPECTED VOLUME OF DATA IN THE DATA POND

Another related and interesting question is: what total volume is expected in each data pond? The answer is that the total volume in any given data pond depends entirely upon the business goals and the nature of data in the business. One industry will have more of one type of data and less of another in their data ponds than another.

An engineering firm or a manufacturing organization is probably going to have lots and lots of analog data. A telephone company is going to have lots of application data. And a marketing research firm is going to have lots of textual data.

Moving Data From Pond to Pond

An interesting architectural question is: once the final state data has been created inside a data pond, can the data be moved to another pond and remain resident in the pond?

The answer is that it is certainly technologically feasible and possible to move data from one data pond to the next and allow that data to remain resident in the source pond. But from an architectural aspect, such a move rarely makes sense. Much of the data pond's value is its supporting infrastructure. In addition to the data in the pond, there is important infrastructure found in the data pond, such as:

- Metadata definitions

- Metaprocess definitions

- Descriptor information.

It is one thing to shuffle data from pond to pond. It is quite another thing to move the infrastructure that supports the data from pond to pond as well. For these reasons, it normally does not make sense to move data outside of the source pond. Fig 9.2 addresses this issue.

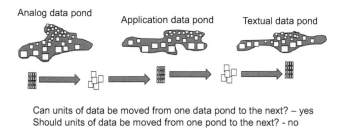

Can units of data be moved from one data pond to the next? – yes
Should units of data be moved from one pond to the next? - no

Fig 9.2 Avoiding data movement from one pond to another

DOING ANALYSIS FROM MULTIPLE PONDS

Another interesting architectural issue is whether it is possible to do analytics based on data found in more than one pond. While possible to do, analytics are usually restricted to the data found in a single pond. This restriction has more to do with the type of data found in the pond and the type of analytics being conducted.

If the analysis requires data from more than one pond, then there is no reason why analytics cannot be done from more than one pond. Fig 9.3 shows the analysis that is conducted from more than one pond and that such analytics are a real possibility.

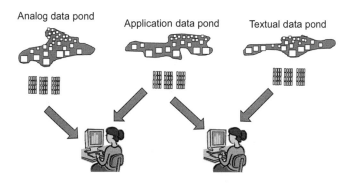

Fig 9.3 Can analysis be done using data from more than one data pond? Yes!

USING METADATA TO RELATE DATA FROM DIFFERENT PONDS

If analyzing data from more than one data pond it is necessary to relate the data from one pond to data in the other. In some cases, this relationship is very quixotic. To facilitate the exchange of data across ponds it is necessary to use the metadata infrastructure.

The metadata for each pond will describe the data in the pond. If it is possible at all to relate data from one pond to another, the relationship is first realized in the metadata. Fig 9.4 shows that when data from different ponds is related, the relationship begins at the metadata level.

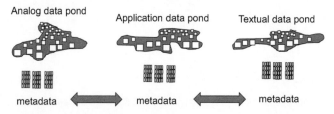

In order for analysis to be done across more than one data pond, there must be synchronization of data at the metadata level before any analysis makes sense

Fig 9.4 Synchronizing metadata is required to analyze across data ponds

WHAT IF...?

Yet another interesting question is what if there is data that is not analog data, not application data, and not textual data that finds its way to the raw data pond? It is certainly possible to have data enter the raw pond that does not fit neatly into one of these three categories. If that is the case, what should be done with the data?

The answer is to *not* try to place the data in a data pond that it does not belong in. That would be a mistake. There are many reasons why this should not be done.

Instead, a good idea is to carve out a part of the raw data pond reserved for data that does not fit into one of the "standard" data ponds. This area can be called the miscellaneous data section of the raw data pond. Fig 9.5 shows the miscellaneous data section of the raw data pond.

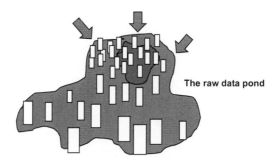

The raw data pond

Fig 9.5 Carving out a miscellaneous data section

The miscellaneous section of the raw data pond can then be used to support business analytical processing, just like other data in the data lake. However, there is a note of caution. The data in the miscellaneous section of the raw data pond must be conditioned in order to support business analytical processing. Fig 9.6 shows the conditioning (transformation and integration) that must be done against data in the miscellaneous data section of the raw data pond.

condition

Fig 9.6 Conditioning must be done against the miscellaneous data section

In Summary

The data lake can be divided up into separate data ponds. Each data pond has its own data and its own characteristics. Seen organically, the data lake and its subdivision of data ponds are seen in Fig 9.7.

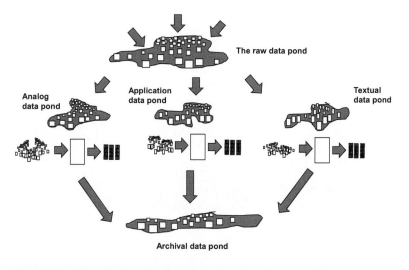

Fig 9.7 Understanding the data pond landscape

Each data pond services its own kind of data and has its own unique analysis that can be performed on data in the pond. In addition, if data is entered into the lake that does not fit into the analog, application, or textual data ponds, then the data can be stored in a special data section of the raw data pond.

Chapter 10
Using the Infrastructure

Nothing elucidates a concept better than an example.

Suppose there was a corporation that had a wide variety of data. The corporation has applications that governed different aspects of their business. There are online systems running transactions that manage the day-to-day interchanges between the corporation and customers. The corporation has data warehouses where corporate analysis is done. The corporation has data marts that are fed by the data warehouse where key performance indicator (KPI) calculations are made periodically.

Yet the corporation also has a lot of other data as well. The firm has competitive data, engineering data, financial data, emails, economic data, tweets, contracts, call center data and a whole host of other data types.

Naturally, the corporation starts to place a lot of its data into a data lake.

After a while, storing data in the lake becomes onerous. Management asks why they are putting information into a data lake when no analysis is being generated from the lake. Or if there is analysis, why is it so slow and expensive?

The organization wakes up to the fact that they have created a "one way" data lake that's more of a liability than an asset.

The "one way" data lake simply does not support business decision making in any meaningful way.

"ONE WAY" DATA LAKE

Fig 10.1 depicts a "one way" data lake that has been built by well-intentioned Big Data developers and data scientists.

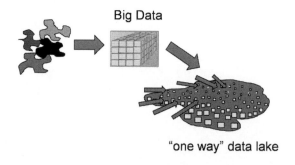

Big Data

"one way" data lake

Fig 10.1 Avoiding the "one way" data lake

One day a manager reads a book describing how to turn the data lake into a positive business asset. The manager understands the problems with the "one way" data lake and decides to build an architected data lake/data pond environment that can truly support decision making in the corporation.

TRANSFORMING THE DATA LAKE

The manager hires a consulting firm and soon they are busily transforming the "one way" data lake into an architected data lake with data ponds. Fig 10.2 shows the data lake/data pond architecture that has been built from the data found in the "one way" data lake.

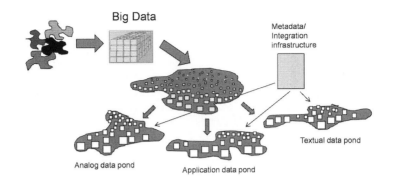

Fig 10.2 Transforming the "one way" data lake into an architected data lake

The newly architected data lake contains three primary data ponds – an analog data pond, and application data pond, and a textual data pond. In addition, there is some small amount of data in the miscellaneous data section of the raw data pond.

TRANSFORMATION TECHNOLOGY

The consulting firm also brings in three distinct technologies for the purpose of transforming/conditioning the raw data in each of the data ponds. For the analog data pond, they use technology that can do data reduction and data compression. For the application data pond, the consulting firm brings in classical ETL technology. And for the textual data pond, they deploy textual disambiguation software. In addition, the consulting firm brings in technology to manage the descriptors, metaprocess information and the metadata that are found in the data lake. Soon the "one way" lake is transformed into a useful tool for the firm.

The transformation process requires work, investment and time. Still, the result is an infrastructure that can really be used for analytical processing. An asset of inestimable value for the corporation.

SOME ANALYTICAL QUESTIONS

As an example of the worth of the architected data lake, consider some simple analytical questions. Suppose the corporation wanted to find out what corporate revenues were for the last quarter. Now suppose the corporation goes and looks in the untransformed/unconditioned data lake environment. In the lake, they have transactions recorded in Australian dollars, Mexican pesos, Canadian dollars, and US dollars.

Certainly the corporation can find the financial transactions. But converting the monetary amounts on the transactions into a common value is a confusing and onerous process that the analyst would rather not have to do. When management wants answers, management wants the answers now. Management does not want to have to wait on complicated calculations and complex analysis.

It is one thing to calculate conversion rates. It is another thing to convert rates as of some moment in time in the past. The conversion calculation is a messy, inaccurate affair. Fig 10.3 shows what management gets when they query the data lake.

But what happens when management queries the architected, integrated data lake/ data pond environment? Since the data has been integrated into a cohesive and accurate number, management quickly gets their answer and has confidence in the value.

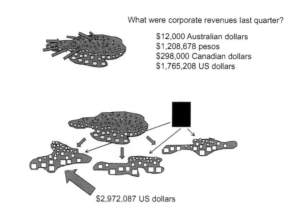

What were corporate revenues last quarter?

$12,000 Australian dollars
$1,208,678 pesos
$298,000 Canadian dollars
$1,765,208 US dollars

$2,972,087 US dollars

Fig 10.3 Querying the data lake

There is no question that building integrated data ponds takes work and investment. But that investment comes back many times over in the analysis that can be performed with the data after it has been architected.

The world of technology has millions of dollars to build things wrong and not a dime to build things right. And this shortsighted attitude comes back to bite the clients more often than the vendors.

Now suppose management has another question to be addressed by the untransformed data lake. Management wants to know how many female employees have taken the SAT exam.

When management looks into the untransformed data lake, they find that every application has encoded the designator for gender differently. One application has encoded women as 0. Other applications have encoded women as F. Another application has encoded women as X, and so forth.

When the applications were built each developer had his/her own way of designating gender. It is one thing to find data. It is another thing to interpret the data accurately. Once again, management just wants answers. They don't want a big explanation about calculations and algorithm processes. But where the applications have not been integrated, management cannot get what it wants. Fig 10.4 shows that access and analysis of unintegrated data is a difficult thing to do.

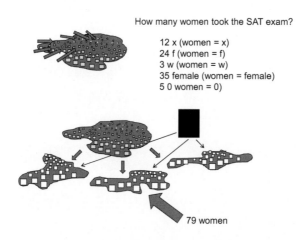

How many women took the SAT exam?

12 x (women = x)
24 f (women = f)
3 w (women = w)
35 female (women = female)
5 0 women = 0)

79 women

Fig 10.4 Challenging queries against unintegrated data

However, when management accesses and analyzes data from the architected, integrated data lake/data pond environment, the answer is easy to locate. In addition to getting the answer quickly, management has confidence that the answer is accurate as well and doesn't have a bunch of asterisks next to the figure.

QUERYING TEXTUAL DATA

Now let's consider another type of data, textual data. Management wishes to know how many books Bill Inmon has written.

Management issues a natural language processing (NLP) query to the data lake. When NLP sees the name "bill" it marks the record. Soon all sorts of "bills" start to appear. There are bird bills. There are billboards. There is an Australian billabong. There is Bill Bryson. They are bills in front of Congress. There are dollar bills. There are hotel bills. And along the way, there are a few references to Bill Inmon.

Doing an un-contextualized query against raw text is very confusing and not very productive. Fig 10.5 shows the confusing query that comes from looking at the untransformed data lake.

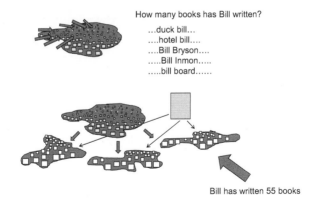

How many books has Bill written?
   ...duck bill...
   ....hotel bill....
   ....Bill Bryson....
   .....Bill Inmon.....
   .....bill board......

Bill has written 55 books

Fig 10.5 Confusing results from the untransformed data lake

But when management looks at the contextualized data in the textual data pond, they see Bill Inmon is the author of 55 books.

Once again, the integration and transformation work done by the creation of a disambiguated textual data pond has paid off in speed of analysis and in terms of confidence of results.

REAL ANALYSIS

The queries and the analysis discussed here are trivial compared to the real analytical queries that organizations do. But these trivial queries are useful in pointing out what the problems of analysis are.

When trying to use an untransformed data lake for analysis the results are confusing and complex. It takes quite an effort to conduct a serious analysis of data in the untransformed data lake. And management does not like long and complex efforts. Fig 10.6 shows that using the untransformed data lake as a basis for analysis is a complex and tedious chore. No wonder the untransformed data lake becomes a "one way" street and turns into a garbage dump.

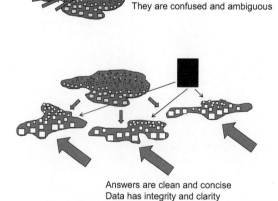

Fig 10.6 Choosing integrity and clarity over ambiguity

It takes time and effort to read, analyze, integrate and condition the data in the data ponds. But that effort turns the data lake into an asset rather than a liability.

In Summary

If you are serious about turning your data lake into a useful corporate asset, you *must* go through the effort and expense of transforming the raw data. The data ponds do the first high-level separation of data into generic data types, and the transformation / conditioning phase turns the data into something that is useful for corporate business analysis.

The alternative to *not* building the data lake/data pond environment is to build a corporate structure that turns into a liability rather than an asset. It's much cheaper to get things right the first time around.

Chapter 11
Search and Analysis

There is much confusion concerning the meaning of analysis and analytics. Obfuscating the marketplace are vendors. Vendors always try to sell their solution as if it were the *only* solution. Vendors don't like architectures because vendors look at an architecture as an obstacle to making a sale. In reality, vendors don't like anything except a sale. Which leads vendors into the bad habit of really confusing customers and the marketplace.

In order to hear a non-vendor influenced discussion on what analysis/analytics are, consider the following. A corporation has a simple desire to find out how many xxxxxxx does yyyyyyy use in a zzzzzzzz time frame. Fig 11.1 depicts this typical analytical question.

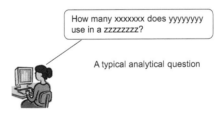

A typical analytical question

Fig 11.1 Answering the typical analytical question

When you stop to analyze the question, it is seen that there are two elements that have been posed:

- Find the data that can be used to answer the question
- Analyze the data once found.

Fig 11.2 shows the two elements of analysis/analytics.

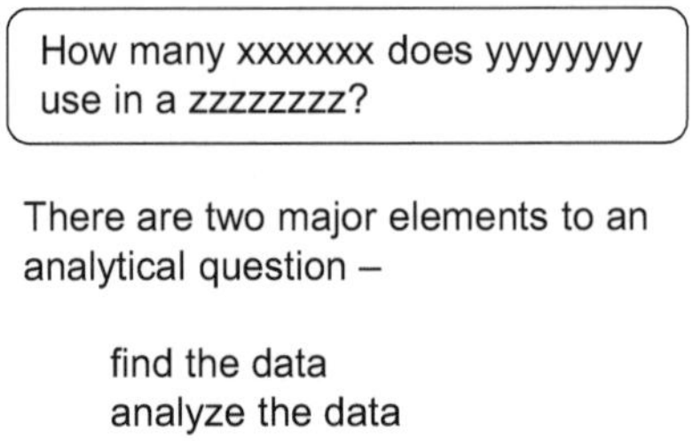

> How many xxxxxxx does yyyyyyy use in a zzzzzzzz?

There are two major elements to an analytical question –

find the data
analyze the data

Fig 11.2 Understanding the two elements of an analytical question

If the criteria for finding the data are straightforward and if the data is indexed, then finding the data is an almost trivial thing to do. But there can arise some complications. Suppose the search is for something that is hidden or disguised, such as encrypted data. Or what if the data is marked by only very faint markers, say for a bank account that was opened fictitiously and has been operated for clandestine purposes. There are many ways data can hide and in these cases, finding data may not be a trivial task at all.

Another way data can hide is by lurking behind a lot of mundane data points. Suppose you wanted to find a particular man in the US and you only knew that he was a man. You would have to search through each male in the US and see if he was the man you were interested in. Such a search would be anything but easy and efficient.

Once the data is found, then it needs to be analyzed. Analyzing data too can be complex. If all data analysis means is to display selected elements of data then analysis is easy. But sometimes analysis of data entails complex algorithms and complex calculations. In any case, there are two very different facets of what is meant by data analysis. Fig 11.3 shows these two sides of the analysis.

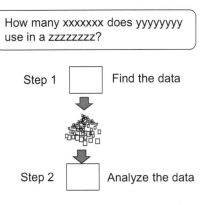

Fig 11.3 Doing data analysis

There are technologies dedicated to these two aspects of analysis. One type is called machine learning and concept search. Machine learning and concept search are dedicated to searching for data where the criteria for searches are murky.

Analysis has the technology of summarization and visualization. Not only is analysis divided up into two distinct facets – search and analysis, but there are different kinds of search. One kind of search looks for very finite sets of data. A person may go looking for the last medical checkup record for Bill Inmon, since there is only one such record at any moment in time.

Or a search may be for a large set of data. Looking for the medical records for a population is one such search. There are many, many medical records for the population of a state or even a city, for example. Fig 11.4 shows that there are different kinds of searches.

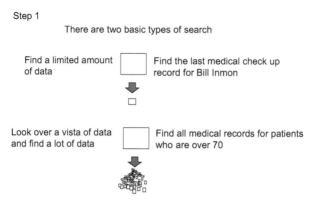

Fig 11.4 Understanding the two basic types of search

The whole subject of doing a search is complicated by the data that is being operated on. When it comes to finding data, the untransformed data lake is very difficult to find anything in. That is because data is very unintegrated inside the untransformed data lake. The lack of data integration inside the untransformed data lake *greatly* contributes to the difficulty of finding data inside the lake. The criteria for searching for data inside the unintegrated data lake are very unclear. The lack of clarity inside the data lake makes for a difficult experience.

But once the data lake becomes integrated, once there are data ponds and the ponds are conditioned, then searches become *much, much* easier and straightforward. Fig 11.5 shows the difference between searching the data lake and searching the conditioned data inside the data ponds.

In fact, there are a lot of reasons why trying to find the right data inside the data lake is so difficult:

- There is so much data that data "hides" or is indistinguishable from other data

- Once you have found something, you are not sure it is actually the data you want
- The criteria for finding data is very unclear
- Even after data has been found, it needs to be converted before it can be used
- The qualifications for data are unclear.

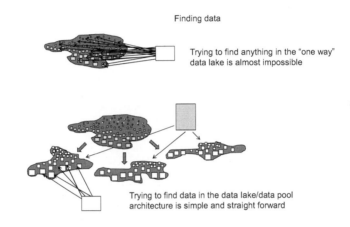

Fig 11.5 Searching the data lake vs. searching the conditioned data inside the data ponds

And data inside the pond – once it has been conditioned – is easy to access and analyze. Fig 11.6 shows why data inside the ponds are suitable for analysis.

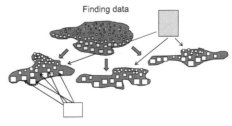

Fig 11.6 Finding data in the data lake is easy for several reasons

After data is found, it's then time to analyze. Data analysis software and technology has been around for a long time, so there are many ways to analyze data once found. Fig 11.7 shows that analysis of data follows after the search.

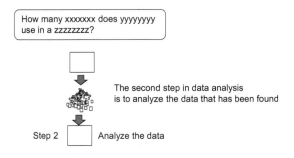

How many xxxxxxx does yyyyyyy use in a zzzzzzzz?

The second step in data analysis is to analyze the data that has been found

Step 2 — Analyze the data

Fig 11.7 Analyzing the data that has been found

There are many forms of analysis. Some of those forms include:

- The mere sorting of data. Sometimes sorting data allows important data to surface and become obvious when that data would not otherwise be so.

- Summarizing data. On occasion, summaries of data bring to light data that would otherwise be lost or overlooked.

- Comparing data. Looking at data and comparing and contrasting to other sets of data often yields insight.

- Exception analysis. Finding outliers and exceptions often lead to insight.

Perhaps the most powerful form of analysis is visualization, studying data in a diagram or picture representation. Visualization is popular because with a properly created visual setup, massive amounts of data can be depicted in such a fashion that important conclusions are immediately obvious. See Fig 11.8.

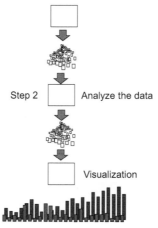

Step 2 — Analyze the data

Visualization

Fig 11.8 Visualizing the data

CONFUSION SPREAD BY THE VENDORS

So how do vendors confuse the marketplace when talking about analysis and analytics?

- Vendors present their product as a final solution when it is only part of a solution

- Vendors hate architecture because it lengthens their sales cycle

- Vendors make assumptions about data that simply are unrealistic

- Vendors confuse search with analysis

- Vendors don't recognize that they are part of a solution.

These are the most common, but there are many other ways that vendors confuse the marketplace. It is in the vendor's best interest to sow seeds of confusion.

IN SUMMARY

There are two aspects to analysis – the search of data and the analysis of that data once the search is complete. The data search is *much* easier and accurate when the search is done against transformed data as found in the data lake/data pond architecture.

Chapter 12
Business Value in the Data Ponds

At the end of the day, if the data lake and data ponds do not provide business value then they will not be supported by the organization for very long. Interestingly, the different data ponds do have potential for providing business value. But the value provided by each data pond and the way that business value is provided are very different.

BUSINESS VALUE IN THE ANALOG DATA POND

The analog data pond can provide business value in one of two manners. There can be a handful of records that are found or there can be patterns of data that are developed across a vista of many records of data.

Consider a company that manufactures airbags for cars. If an airbag malfunctions, there can be very serious consequences. Suppose an accident occurs where an airbag does not go off. The accident investigator finds the manufacturer of the airbag. Then the investigator determines that the airbag was manufactured in March 1995 at the Phoenix, Arizona facility. The company now looks back into their analog data and finds all other airbags that were manufactured in March and April of 1995 and alerts the owners of the cars that have these airbags to have their airbags checked, thus avoiding a potentially serious consequence. In this case, the analog data was examined to find a handful of records that had potentially very serious consequences.

Another business value of analog data is looking across large vistas of data in a hurry. One day, management wishes to rethink the way an airbag is manufactured because there is a new technology that triggers an airbag more efficiently and safely. The manufacturer looks at a massive amount of analog data to determine just how many airbags there are with the older firing mechanism. Fig 12.1 shows these two business values of the usage of analog data.

Business value

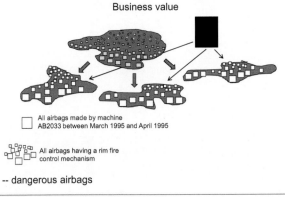

All airbags made by machine
AB2033 between March 1995 and April 1995

All airbags having a rim fire
control mechanism

-- dangerous airbags

Fig 12.1 Benefiting from analog data

As another example of finding a few valuable records, consider telephone call record detail records. One day the government finds telephone calls between terrorists. There may be millions and millions of telephone call detail records, but only a handful of those are from terrorists. There is no question of the value of being able to identify terrorists and thereby preventing acts of terrorism. In this case, many, many records are examined in the hopes of finding just a handful of records.

Looking across vistas of data is a different matter altogether. Instead of looking for a few points out of many, the analyst is looking for patterns of data which are manifest across many, many records. As an example of looking for patterns, the analyst may find that certain equipment starts to malfunction or function in a less than accurate fashion towards the end of the month. Upon further investigation, it is found that maintenance to equipment is done on the first of the month. By month's end, the machinery needs to be recalibrated and cleaned. This important pattern of data is detected not just by scouring records, but by using their metaprocess information in conjunction with the records themselves. Fig 12.2 shows the types of business value that can be derived from the analog data pond.

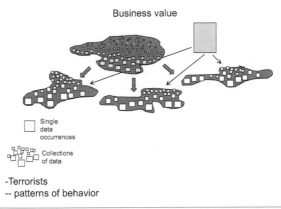

Fig 12.2 Types of business value derived from the analog data pond

BUSINESS VALUE IN THE APPLICATION DATA POND

Finding business value from the application data pond is a different proposition. Some typical examples of finding business value are locating a particular receipt or the determination of the average cost of shipments for 1999.

Suppose the organization is going through an audit and they are looking for documentation from a previous year. The document is needed to prove to an auditor an expense item. The operational systems only go back three years, but the audit is for five years ago. The organization looks to its application data pond to find the receipt. In this case, there was a search across many documents in the hope of finding just one. In another circumstance, management thinks that shipment costs are rising too quickly. In order to get a historical perspective on costs, management goes back to 1999 to calculate shipment costs. They find those shipment costs in the application data pond. In order to determine annual shipment costs, a calculation must be done using many, many documents. Fig 12.3 shows the type of business value that can be derived from the application data pond.

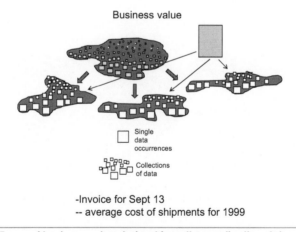

Business value

☐ Single data occurrences

Collections of data

-Invoice for Sept 13
-- average cost of shipments for 1999

Fig 12.3 Types of business value derived from the application data pond

BUSINESS VALUE IN THE TEXTUAL DATA POND

Yet a third type of business value can be derived from the textual data pond. Suppose that a price has been agreed upon for an order. However, the only documentation is in writing – in a paper letter. The organization searches the entire textual data pond in order to find one document.

Yet another kind of business value that can be derived from the textual data pond is determining customer sentiment. Customer sentiment is expressed in many ways – through tweets, through emails, through other forms of narration.

The organization reads and stores these documents in their textual data pond, which then passes these documents through textual disambiguation and creates a database that can be analyzed, making it easy to determine customer sentiment.

Customer sentiment is gauged by looking at many documents, reading and disambiguating the contents of the documents, and placing the results in a database, where analysis can be performed. Knowing customer sentiment is an extremely valuable thing for the business. Fig 12.4 depicts the business value that can be derived from the textual data pond.

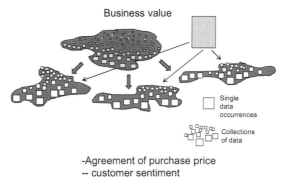

Fig 12.4 Types of business value derived from the textual data pond

PERCENT OF RECORDS THAT HAVE BUSINESS VALUE

Another interesting way of looking at business value provided by the different data ponds is through the percentage of records that have business value.

Some data points have records that have a very high percentage of business value. Other data have records with a very low percentage of data value. Consider telephone calls.

In the US each day, there are millions of telephone calls made. If a person were looking for telephone calls made by terrorists, it is safe to say that there are only a handful of relevant points. In fact, on any given day there may be no telephone calls made by terrorists. When you look at the percentage of terrorist telephone calls made each day versus the total number of calls, the percentage is *very* low. Perhaps the percentage is as low as .0000001%. And the same very low percentages of records holding business value hold true for such things as log tapes, click stream records, and lots of other data.

Now consider other types of data, like textual data. Textual data is gathered from places like call center conversations, customer feedback, and so forth. Each phone call represents a customer's concerns or message. The content of each phone call has real business value.

For most of textual data, 100% of the data has business value. Admittedly, some phone conversations have more value than others. But *every* telephone conversation has *some* business value.

There is then a stark difference between the percentage of records that have business value in the data ponds. Fig 12.5 depicts these value differences.

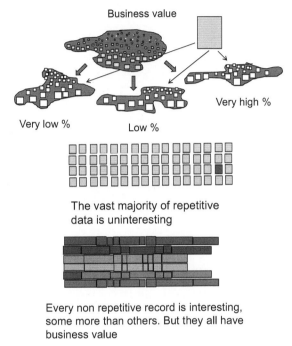

Fig 12.5 Understanding the value of data in the various types of data ponds

IN SUMMARY

There are two types of business value found in the data ponds. Most data value is found in a very small number of records, though high value data is often found in vast vistas of low value data.

In general, repetitive data has a very low percentage of records that contain business value, whereas non-repetitive records have a very high percentage of records that have business value.

Chapter 13
Additional Topics

Documentation is included in any computerized system. Documentation is especially important for the data lake/data pond environment. Without documentation, the analyst trying to use the data lake/data pond environment will not be successful. Documentation is absolutely essential for success in the data lake/data pond environment.

HIGH SYSTEM LEVEL DOCUMENTATION

There are at least two levels of documentation which are necessary for the data lake/data pond environment. One crucial point is the high system level. At the high system level there is documentation about:

- How data enters the data lake and/or data pond

- How data flows from one data pond to the next

- How data flows into the archival data pond environment.

The high system level documentation for the data pond then shows the business analyst the general flow of data within the data lake/data pond environment.

DETAILED DATA POND LEVEL DOCUMENTATION

The second level of necessary documentation is documentation at the detailed data pond level. The type of documentation that is needed here covers:

- Metadata of the data found in the data pond
- Metaprocess information about the activities taking place in the data pond
- Transformation documentation
- An architectural description of the flow of data within the data pond
- The criteria for selection for entry into the data pond
- The criteria for exit out of the data pond.

Once the business analyst finds the general place where his/her data is, they then need to have detailed information about how to access and manipulate data accurately. The low level of documentation provides this detailed information.

WHAT DATA FLOWS INTO THE DATA LAKE/DATA POND?

In Fig 13.1, there is the familiar corporate information factory, where the application/operational systems, the data warehouse and data marts, and other structures of data are found. But there is a host of other data in the corporation that is not found in the corporate information factory. There is also external data. There is analog data. There is security data. There is textual data, and so forth.

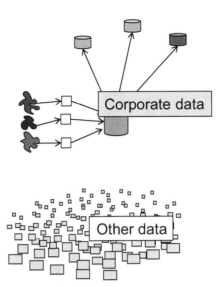

Fig 13.1 Expanding the corporate information factory

Fig 13.2 shows that the two sources of data feed the data lake/data pond environment.

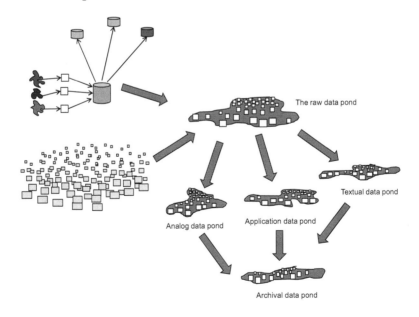

Fig 13.2 Focusing in on the data relationships

WHERE DOES ANALYSIS OCCUR?

Looking at the diagram seen in Fig 13.2, it's now an interesting question to ask: where do different kinds of analysis occur? The organization conducts all sorts of analysis. Some is online in real time. Some of the analysis is for corporate historical data. Some analysis is KPI analysis or textual information.

So it is instructive to ask, what kind of analysis occurs where? Fig 13.3 shows that online, real time analysis takes place in the applications. Activities such as bank transactions, airline reservations, manufacturing control activities, shipment recording and so forth occur here. The activity is online and real time, occurring in a matter of seconds. Typically, only a very small amount of data is accessed though. Updates and insert processing usually occur here.

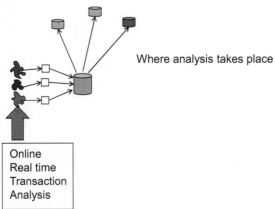

Where analysis takes place

Online
Real time
Transaction
Analysis

Fig 13.3 Analyzing online real time

The corporate analytical location is the data warehouse, as seen in Fig 13.4. Data from different applications is integrated into the data warehouse. Typically, 3 to 5 years' worth of history is stored here. The analytical processing that occurs is performed in ranges from 5 minutes to 24 hours. In order to get the data into the data warehouse, it passes through ETL (extract/transform/load) processing. As data passes from the application environment to the data warehouse through extract/transform/load processing, the data is then transformed from an application state to a corporate state.

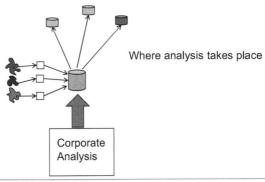

Fig 13.4 Sourcing data for analysis from the data warehouse

Surrounding the data warehouse are data marts. Data marts are where KPI analysis occurs, typically on a departmental basis. Marketing, sales, finance and so forth all have their own KPI's. Fig 13.5 depicts the data mart processing and analysis found in the corporate information factory.

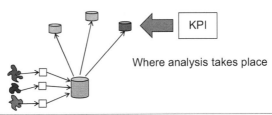

Fig 13.5 Sourcing data for analysis from the corporate information factory

Various and sundry other processing and analysis occurs outside the corporate information factory. Most often, the processing is very detailed and immediate. There are the reading of meters, the control of manufacturing devices, and the electronic eye reading of vehicles passing a control point. Fig 13.6 shows the kind of processing and analysis that occurs outside the corporate information factory.

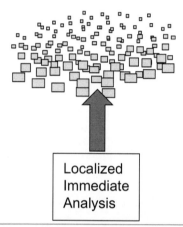

Fig 13.6 Processing and analyzing data outside the corporate information factory

And finally, there is the analytical processing that occurs in the data lake/data pond environment. The most common forms of analytical processing on the data found in the data lake/data pond environment are pattern discovery and deep historical analysis.

In the textual data pond, sentiment analysis occurs as well. Fig 13.7 shows the analytical processing that occurs in the data lake/data pond environment.

There are then many different kinds of analytical activities occurring across the information landscape of the corporation. Analysis in one place is usually quite different than the analysis elsewhere.

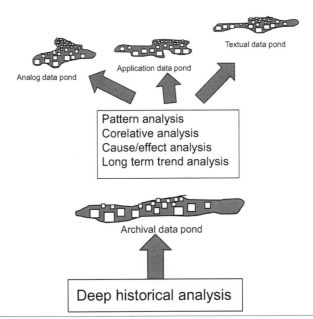

Fig 13.7 Analyzing data by applying various processing techniques

THE AGE OF DATA

Another interesting question is, what is the age of data in the data lake/data pond environment? The answer is that data of *any* age can be found in the data lake/data pond environment.

Normally, data that is very fresh – seconds old – is found in the operational environment. Data that is from one year to five years old is found in the data warehouse/data mart environment. And data that is of *any* age is found in the data lake/data pond environment.

The data lake is the original long-term carrier of data.

On occasion, information is kept simply because it is cheaper to store the data than it is to ever have to recreate the data again. The theory is that if the data was important enough to be captured electronically in the first place, then the data is important enough to never have to be recreated again. There may be no foreseeable need for the data but the data is kept in any case.

Another reason to keep data for lengthy periods of time are statutory requirements. Some data must be kept forever because of legal mandate. Storing that data in the data lake/data pond environment is a good thing to do.

SECURITY OF DATA

Data in the data lake/data pond environment needs security, just like the other parts of the data processing environment. However, the security criticality of the data lake/data pond environment is somewhat less than the security criticality of the other parts of the data processing environment. That is because of the timeliness of the data. Data in the data lake/data pond environment is likely to be much older than the data found elsewhere in the data processing environment.

IN SUMMARY

Documentation is an important part of the data lake/data pond environment. There are two levels of documentation required. There is high-level system documentation and there is low-level documentation.

Data flows into the data lake/data pond from two basic places – the corporate information factory and other data.

Different kinds of analysis occur in different locations. Online analysis takes place in the online operational systems. Corporate data analysis occurs in the data warehouse. KPI analysis occurs in the data mart. Limited immediate analysis is conducted in the miscellaneous data found elsewhere.

The data lake/data pond supports different kinds of analysis.

The age of data kept in the data lake/data pond environment is very lengthy.

The data lake/data pond environment requires security, but not the stringent level of security that is found elsewhere in the data processing environment.

Chapter 14
Analytical and Integration Tools

There are a variety of tools that support the data lake/data pond environment. Each provides a different functionality that is needed in the data lake/data pond environment. Some of the most prominent tools will be mentioned here.

VISUALIZATION

Visualization is the technology that takes data (usually in a relational format), organizes and displays the data. By turning details in a database into a visualization, the organization can immediately see patterns and trends that would not otherwise be obvious. Visualization is especially useful to non-technical management.

In many cases, management cannot understand what is being said unless the data is visualized.

Visualization technology can organize data in a variety of forms. Visualization can create Pareto charts, pie charts and scatter charts, among other forms of visualization.

In order to be effective, the data going into a visualization needs to be organized into a database format first. Most visualization technology requires that the data it operates on be stored in a relational database format. Fig 14.1 shows some visualizations.

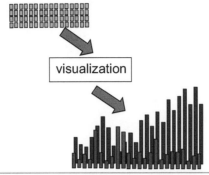

Fig 14.1 Visualizing data that is sourced from a relational database

SEARCH AND QUALIFY

Another useful and sophisticated technology is search and qualify technology. Some search technology is quite simple, whereas others are very sophisticated. Search and qualify technology can do sophisticated searches where data may be less than optimally organized, such as against textual data.

One of the sophisticated forms of search technology is the machine learning and concept search technology. In the machine learning and concept search technology, textual documents can be read and qualified. The qualification of the documents is done in an extremely sophisticated manner.

Suppose that a company had an account code named "rawhide." Search and qualify technology makes the term rawhide stand out because when mentioned, there never are terms that are normally associated with leather found near rawhide. There is no mention of saddles, or ropes or Mexican riatas or any of the terms you might expect to be associated with real rawhide. Instead, rawhide is a term that means something unique. Fig 14.2 shows search and qualify technology.

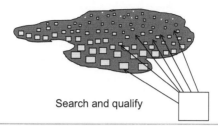

Search and qualify

Fig 14.2 Searching and qualifying technology

TEXTUAL DISAMBIGUATION

A most useful technology in the textual data pond is the technology known as textual disambiguation. In textual disambiguation technology, raw textual narration is read and converted to a standard database format. In addition, the context of the text is identified and written along with the text. Textual disambiguation is complex technology. It deals with language and language is inherently complicated. For those organizations doing serious textual analysis, textual disambiguation is an absolute necessity. Fig 14.3 shows the role of textual disambiguation.

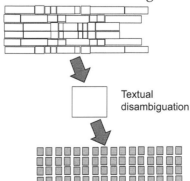

Textual disambiguation

Fig 14.3 Applying textual disambiguation

STATISTICAL ANALYSIS

Statistical analysis is another technology that is quite useful for reading masses of data and doing sophisticated statistical analysis of the data.

Statistical analysis entails not only the calculation of analytical numbers, but the graphical display of those numbers in a meaningful manner. Fig 14.4 depicts statistical analysis.

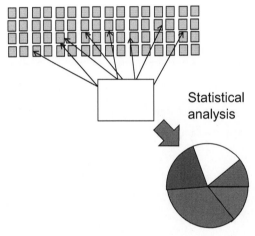

Fig 14.4 Applying statistical analysis

CLASSICAL ETL PROCESSING

Classical ETL is useful for reading and integrating application data, and therefore the transformation process. Classical ETL processing reads application-based data and turns it into corporate data that has been integrated. Fig 14.5 shows classical ETL technology.

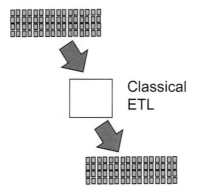

Fig 14.5 Understanding ETL technology

In Summary

There are several technologies which are helpful for building and supporting the data lake/data pond environment. Some of these technologies are:

- Visualization
- Search and qualify
- Textual disambiguation
- Statistical analysis
- Classical ETL

Chapter 15
Archiving Data Ponds

An essential part of the data lake/data pond architecture is the archival data pond. The archival data pond is fed from data from the analog data pond, the application data pond and the textual data pond. Fig 15.1 shows the archival data pond.

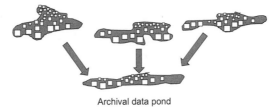

Archival data pond

Fig 15.1 Understanding the archival data pond

The archival data pond is used to hold data whose probable useful life has diminished. The purpose of this pond is:

- To have a place to store data that *might* have some future use
- To allow useless data to be removed from data ponds so that analysis in those data ponds can proceed in an efficient manner.

CRITERIA FOR REMOVAL

There are several criteria for the removal of data from the analog, application and textual data ponds. Some critical ones are:

- The aging of data.

- The lowering of the probability of usage.

- The need to store data because of litigated activity.

- The need to store data because of the criticality regardless of the probability of access.

STRUCTURAL ALTERATION

As data is being restructured from the data ponds to the archival data pond, a structural change to the data occurs. Data in the archival data pond has both metadata and metaprocess information attached directly to the raw data. This attachment ensures that when future analysts go looking through the archival data, then that metadata and metaprocess information is not lost. Fig 15.2 shows the restructuring that occurs as data is moved into the archival data pond.

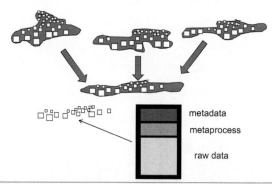

metadata

metaprocess

raw data

Fig 15.2 Restructuring as data is moved into the archival data pond

Once data is placed in the archival data pond, it is often useful to index the data independently so that future analysts will be able to find data efficiently.

CREATING INDEPENDENT INDEXES FOR ARCHIVAL DATA

Fig 15.3 shows the indexing of data in the archival data pond.

Archival data

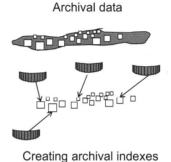

Creating archival indexes

Fig 15.3 Indexing of data in the archival data pond

IN SUMMARY

The archival data pond receives data from the other data ponds when the data in those ponds has a very low probability of usage. Data in the data archival pond is held in the pond indefinitely. Data is restructured as it enters the archival data pond in order to have metadata and metaprocess information placed physically adjacent to the actual data itself. On occasion, separate and independent indexes of data are created and stored in the data archival pond.

Glossary

4GL – fourth generation language – a computer language optimized for ease of use

Acronym resolution – the process of expanding acronyms into their literal meaning

Alternate spelling – a different way of forming a word pattern

Alternate storage – storage other than disk based storage used to hold bulk amounts of data

Analog – a type of computing driven by sensory perceptions and signals, as opposed to a digital computer

Analog data pond – the data pond where analog data is placed and processed

Application – a computerized system dedicated to solving or empowering a specific business function

Application data pond – the subset of the architected integrated data lake where application data is stored and processed

Archival database – a collection of data containing information of a historical nature

Archival processing – the activities surrounding older and/or inactive data

Archival data pool – a component of the architected integrated data lake environment where data is passed when the probability of access is close to zero

Big Data – the storage of massive amounts of data in inexpensive storage

Business process – a synonym for value chain, the term used to differentiate a value chain of activities from a functional process or functional set of activities

Business rule – a statement expressing a policy, guideline or condition that governs business activities and or business decisions

CIF – corporate information factory – the data warehouse centric architecture that contains operational sources of data, ETL, an ODS and data marts

Conditioning – the transformation process that data in the data ponds pass through

Constraint – the business rule that places a restriction on business actions and/or decisions

Contextualization – the process of identifying the context of a word

Database – a structured collection of units of data organized around some topic or theme

Data lake – the place Big Data is stored

Data pond – a subdivision of the architected integrated data lake

Data scientist – an individual dedicated to the study of patterns found in data

DBMS – database management system – system software that manages the storage and access of data on disk storage

Document – a basic unit of textual data

Great divide – the division of Big Data between repetitive data and non-repetitive data

Hadoop – technology designed to house Big Data – a framework for managing data

Homograph – a word or phrase whose interpretation depends on the person who originally wrote the word or phrase

Homographic resolution – the process of contextualizing data based on the identity of the person who uttered the text

Inline contextualization – the technique of inferring context by establishing a beginning delimiter and an ending delimiter

Log tape – A sequential record of the activities that have occurred inside a system. Sometimes called a "journal" tape. The primary purpose of a log tape is for backup and recovery of a system.

Logical data model – a data model based on inferred relationships

Metadata – the classic definition of metadata as "data about the data."

Non-repetitive data – data whose records have no predictable pattern of structure or content. Typical non-repetitive records include email, call center data, warranty claim data, insurance claim data, and so forth

Parsing – the process of reading text and finding contextualized value that resides in the text

Pattern analysis – the analysis that seeks to find recognizable patterns in the occurrence of points of data

Proximity analysis – an analysis based on the closeness of words or taxonomies to each other

Statistical analysis – the process of looking at a large number of values and evaluating the values mathematically

Stop word – a word in a language that is needed for communication but not needed to convey information. In English there are stop words such as "a," "and," "the," "to," "from" and so forth

Structured data – data that is managed by a database management system

Taxonomy – a classification of text

Textual data pond – the subset of the architected integrated data lake where textual data is stored and processed

Textual disambiguation – the process of reading text and formatting text into a standard database format

References

Data Architecture

Data Architecture – A Primer for the Data Scientist, W H Inmon, 2013, Elsevier Kauffman, Boston. Mass.

Data Architecture: The Information Paradigm, W H Inmon, QED, Wellesley, MA, 1998.

DW 2.0 – Architecture for the Next Generation of Data Warehousing, W H, Inmon, June 2008.

Information Systems Architecture: A System Developers Primer, W H Inmon, Prentice Hall, Englewood Cliffs, NJ 1981.

Information Systems Architecture: Development in the 90's, W H Inmon, John Wiley 1992.

Information Systems Architecture, W H Inmon, QED, WELLESLEY, MA 1986.

The Government Information Factory, W H Inmon, IDS, Denver, CO 80109.

Data Warehouse

Building the Data Warehouse, First Edition, W H Inmon, QED, Wellesley, MA, 1990.

Building the Unstructured Data Warehouse, W H Inmon, Technics Publications, 2011.

Data Warehousing and Decision Support, W H Inmon, Spiral Books, Manchester, NH 1997.

Data Warehousing for E-Business, W H Inmon, John Wiley, NY NY 2001.

Data Warehouse Performance, W H Inmon, John Wiley and Sons, 1999.

Managing The Data Warehouse, W H Inmon, John Wiley and Sons (1997).

Using The Data Warehouse, W H Inmon, John Wiley and Sons 1994.

Data Warehouse in the Age of Big Data, Krish Krishnan, Morgan Kaufmann, 2005.

Social Data Analytics, Krish Krishnan, Morgan Kaufmann, 2009.

Data Warehouse Project Management, Sid Adelman, Larissa Moss, Addison-Wesley, 2000.

Building a Scalable Data Warehouse with Data Vault 2.0, Dan Linstedt, Morgan Kaufmann, 2015.

Modelling the Agile Data Warehouse With Data Vault, Hans Hultgren, New Hamilton, 2012.

Business of Data Vault Modelling, Dan Linstedt, Kent Graziano, 2010.

Corporate Information Factory

Building the Operational Data Store, W H Inmon, John Wiley 1999.

Business Metadata, W H Inmon Elsevier Press, Aug 2007.

Data Model Resource Book, W H Inmon John Wiley and Sons, NY NY, 1997.

Data Stores, Data Warehousing and the Zachman Framework, W H Inmon, McGraw-Hill, NY NY 1997.

Exploration Warehousing: Turning Information into Business Opportunity, W H Inmon, John Wiley 2000.

The Corporate Information Factory, W H Inmon, First Edition, John Wiley, 1998.

Analytics

Data Pattern Processing: the Key to Competitive Advantage, John Wiley, NY, NY, 1990

Tapping Into Unstructured Data, W H Inmon, Prentice Hall, 2007, with Tony Nesavich

Data Marts

The Data Warehouse Toolkit, Ralph Kimball, John Wiley and Sons, 1997.

The Kimball Group Reader, Ralph Kimball, John Wiley, 2005.

Lifecycle Toolkit, Ralph Kimball, John Wiley, 2000.

Web Sites of Interest

WWW.Forestrimtech.com, a web site with white papers about textual disambiguation and other data architecture topics

Index